Flute

Mary Karen Clardy
Flute Fundamentals II
The Art of the Phrase

ED 30019
ISMN M-60001-054-7
ISBN 978-1-4234-8115-7
Series Editor: Scott Wollschleger
Cover: Photograph by steverileypictures.com

www.schott-music.com

Mainz · London · Madrid · New York · Paris · Prague · Tokyo · Toronto

Dedication

This book is dedicated to my students, an endless source of joy and inspiration in a lifelong pursuit of the art of music.

"Music produces a kind of pleasure which mankind cannot do without."

Confucius
(c. 551-479 BC)

"Without music, life would be a mistake."

Friedrich Nietzche
(1844-1900)

Preface

"Music, to be an art, must flow from inspiration, not mechanism."

Franz Liszt
(1811-1886)

Renowned for his virtuoso technique, the eminent 19th century pianist and composer Franz Liszt recognized the need for musical artistry beyond a strictly mechanical approach. Phrasing adds content to pitch and rhythm. The art of music is found in the connections within a phrase. Often overlooked by young players, attention to musical content helps solve technical issues, develops breath control, and builds confidence in a flutist. Simple rules establish fundamentals of tone production and phrasing, but the acoustic principles of the flute require constant attention to create sound, sustain notes, and maintain phrase direction. Repetitive and mindless practice encourages incorrect physical habits. It is essential to add musical content to the printed notes and rhythms. Flute study should be a simultaneous process of developing musical phrasing and building technical skill, with simple melodies included in daily practice to encourage and develop confidence in phrasing.

Now in its 5th printing, **Flute Fundamentals** *The Building Blocks of Technique* (EA 730, 1992) continues to gain recognition after almost two decades in print. This second volume **Flute Fundamentals II** *The Art of the Phrase* (ED 30015, 2009) continues and expands the basic concepts with added exercises for development of musical phrasing, content, and expression. The musical excerpts in this volume are taken from orchestral and solo repertoire, providing inspiration and enjoyment when practicing *The Art of the Phrase*.

Mary Karen Clardy
Dallas, 2009

Contents

CHAPTER 1
Musical Notation

Musical notation represents pitch and duration along with other details of key signature, meter, tempo, expression, and dynamics. The visual appearance of notes encourages separation of pitches rather than connection into phrases. Replacing printed notes with horizontal bars encourages a consistent air column necessary for flow and direction in phrasing. The process of seeing a note, hearing the pitch, then creating music from the symbol of notation is essential at every stage; and as the building blocks of music, daily scale practice helps develop a natural sense of phrasing within the perfect melody of the scale. Memorizing scales eliminates the restriction of reading, allowing for creative practice that includes patterns, transpositions, articulations, dynamics, and rhythms. Maintain smooth finger movements through note changes, preparing for the next scale degree with the internal ear and a supportive air column. Mechanical finger movements limit phrase direction, creating vertical sounds that restrict flow in phrasing. It's important to remember that music exists only when the printed page is brought to life by a performer.

Scale Exercises

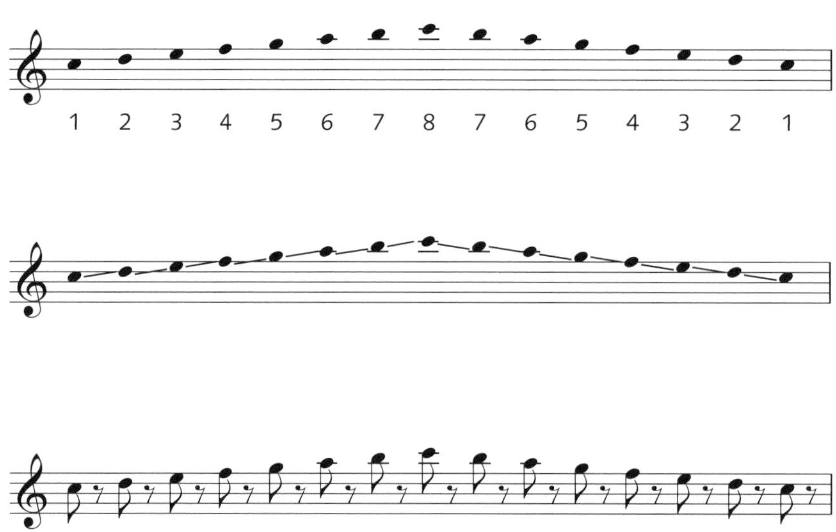

Practice scales with phrase direction and a constant air flow throughout the scale degrees for color and shape. Memorize and transpose the scale pattern to all twelve keys as an ear training exercise, replacing note heads with horizontal bars to visualize phrase connections. Add rests between scale degrees to strengthen internal pulse and develop rhythmic accuracy.

Musical Excerpts

Christoph Willibald von Gluck
Orfeo ed Euridice (1762), Minuet of the Blessed Spirits, mm. 1-8

Lento
dolciss.
p

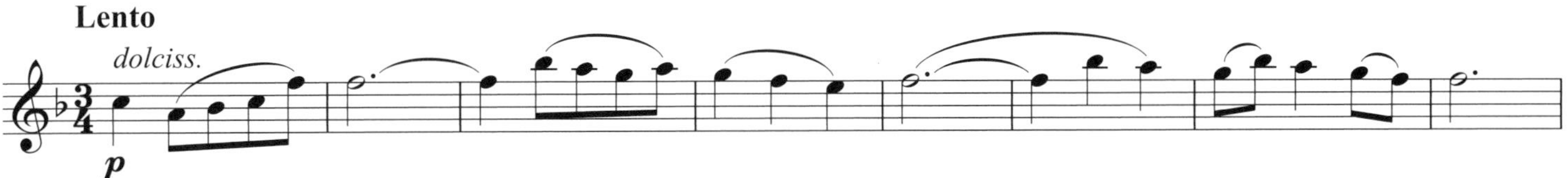

In this beautiful example of lyric style think of singing the melody. Shape the phrase with the natural rise and fall of the line. Connect the notes with smooth finger changes.

Camille Saint-Saëns
Le Carnaval des Animaux (1886), movement 13, *Le Cygne*, mm. 1-27

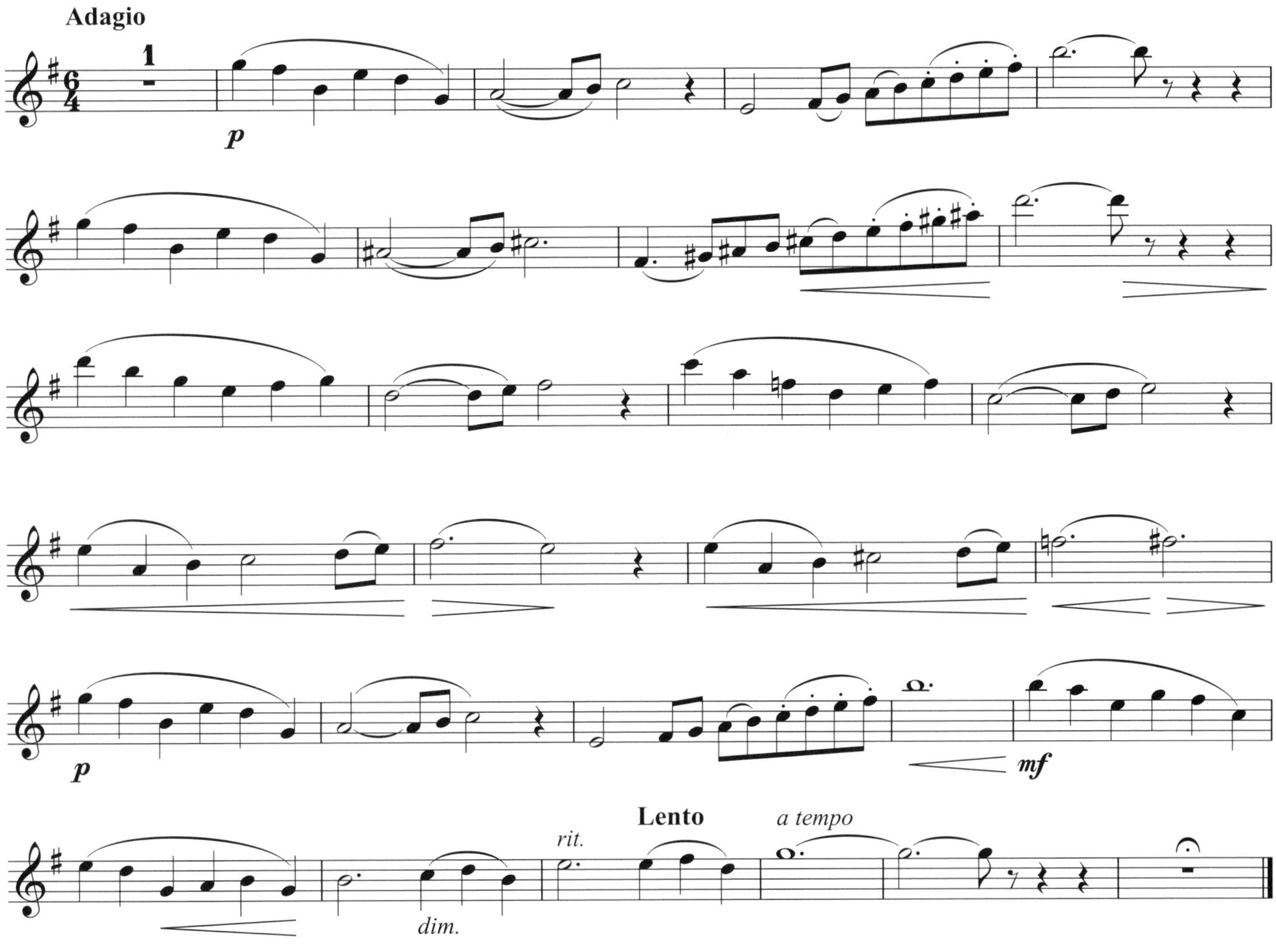

Adagio
1
p
p
mf
rit.
Lento
a tempo
dim.

This music was originally scored for the cello. Energize the air column to create direction and color in the phrases as a cellist uses the bow to connect the line.

Antonín Dvorák
Symphony No. 9 in E Minor, op. 95 (From the New World), movement 1, mm. 91-99, Flutes 1&2

Antonín Dvorák
Symphony No. 9 in E Minor, op. 95 (From the New World), movement 1, mm. 316-336

This familiar theme appears throughout the *New World Symphony* with transformation through transposition, dynamics, articulation change, and the scoring in both flute parts. Memorize these examples. Then transpose to other keys as an ear training exercise. This will also help build confidence with memory.

Georges Bizet
L'Arlésienne Suite No. 2, op. 23, movement 1, *Pastorale*, mm. 58-76

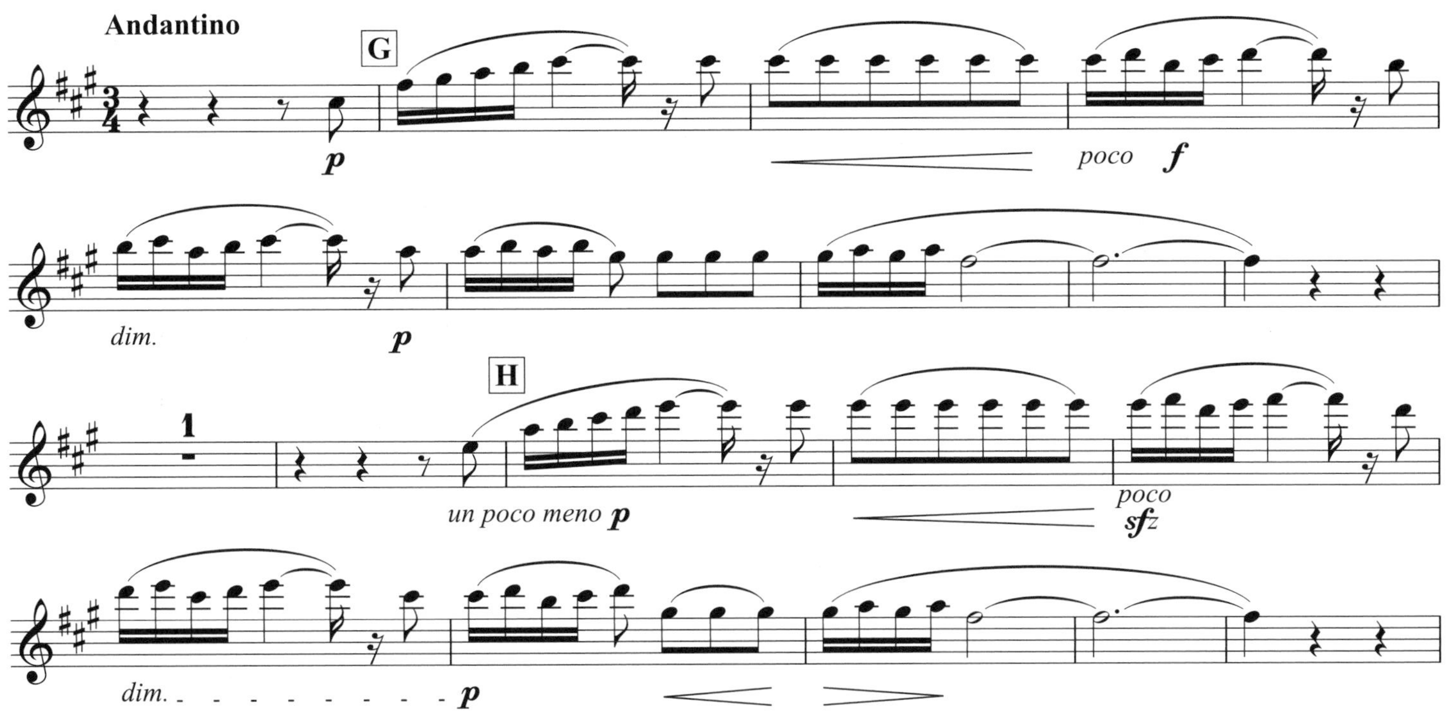

In this passage Bizet uses both the minor and relative major versions of the theme with a dramatic color change. For variety in practice begin with the major theme and follow with the minor version.

Georges Bizet
L'Arlésienne Suite No. 2, op. 23, movement 4, *Farandole*, mm. 84-124

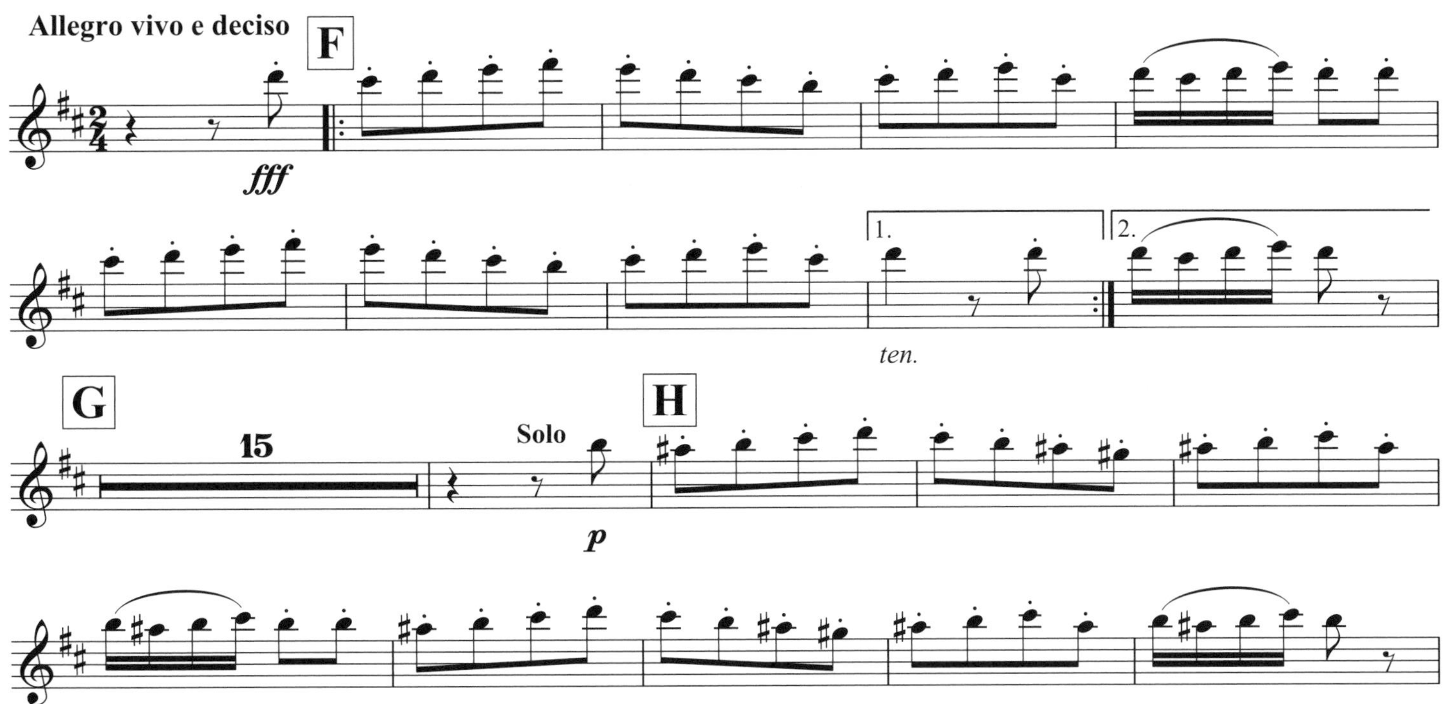

In contrast with the previous excerpt, the major and relative minor versions of the theme are reversed. Concentrate on keeping hands and fingers loose for smooth phrasing in staccato scale patterns.

CHAPTER 2
Breathing

As the simplest wind instrument the flute needs a consistent and energetic air flow for sound production. Both quantity and quality of breath are necessary to sustain phrases, create direction, and add color to music. Think of singing or whistling behind the finger changes along with the image of pedaling a bicycle to help create a feeling of forward movement in phrases. Breathing exercises belong in every flutist's daily routine to encourage relaxed, normal breathing and to build good habits for musical phrasing. Shallow breaths create tension, restrict phrasing and limit confidence in performance. On the other hand, deep breaths provide energy, flow, and direction in phrasing. Try exhaling completely before inhaling. The result is often a calmer, deeper breath. The body should be relaxed and expanded for maximum intake. Slow, deep breathing fills the body with the quantity of air necessary for a phrase. Attention to good breathing habits minimizes breath control issues. Remember to breathe deeply at the beginning of each phrase. Hear the pitch and establish the meter before playing the first note. Plan breaths at phrase points; coordinating capacity with phrase length, spinning the phrase forward to the next breath while maintaining musical integrity through the last note of the phrase.

Breathing Exercises

Practice daily long tones with the metronome at ♩ = 60. Gradually increase the length of the notes while following these simple suggestions to develop breath capacity and control.

1) Think of the air column as an elevator in a tall building, moving down for inhalation and up for exhalation.

2) Spin the air column through the long tones and think of blowing out a candle when approaching the breath, creating a seamless phrase as the body naturally fills again with air.

3) Relax the upper body and throat through end of the phrase, the breath, and beginning of the next phrase.

Musical Excerpts

Georges Bizet
Carmen Entr'acte, before Act III

One of the most beautiful solos in orchestral repertoire, *Entr'acte* provides the flutist with a unique opportunity to develop breath capacity and control through the natural sense of phrasing found in Bizet's music. Practice the excerpt in smaller units to develop confidence, then combine the smaller phrases for a polished, artistic performance.

Ludwig van Beethoven
Leonore Overture No. 3, op. 72a, mm. 1-5

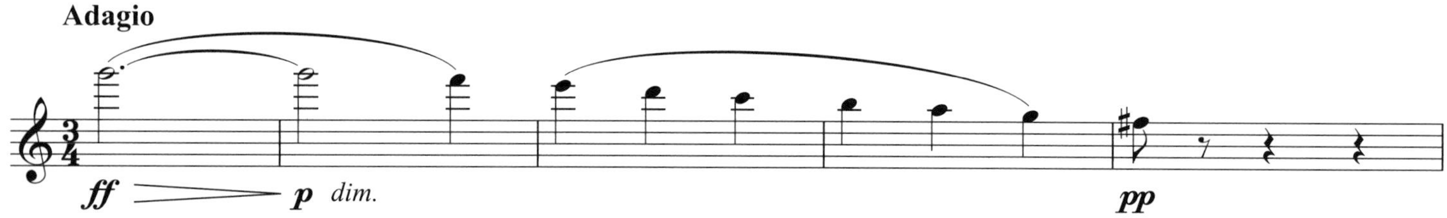

The opening of Beethoven's *Leonore Overture* No. 3 should be performed in one breath. Develop breath control by practicing the excerpt at a faster tempo. Adjust to a slower tempo as capacity and confidence increase.

Gioachino Rossini
Guillaume Tell (1829), Overture, mm. 176-195

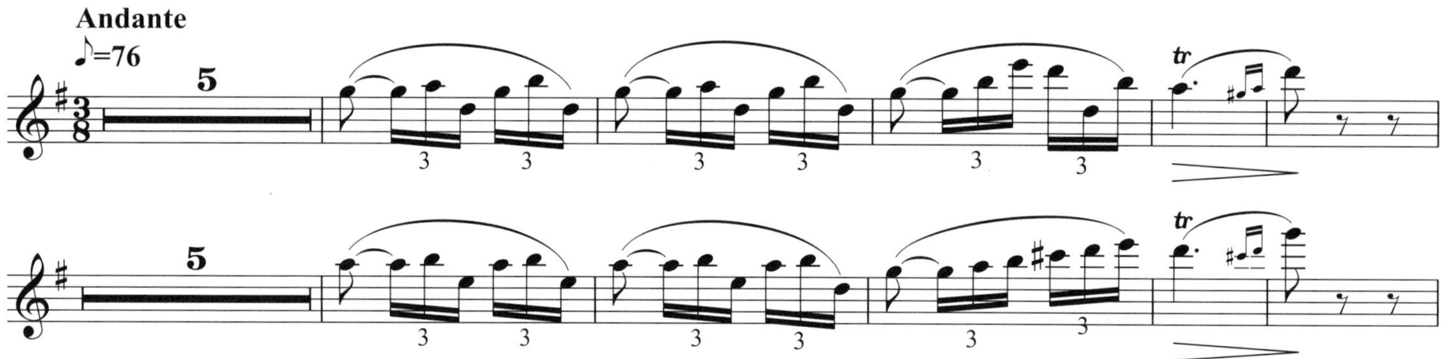

These solos should be performed in one breath. It's helpful to practice the last three measures of the solo to build confidence with breath control. Add the preceding measures one at a time to develop capacity and phrasing.

Claude Debussy
Prélude à L'Après-midi d'un faune (1876), mm. 1-4

This passage is perhaps the most difficult orchestral excerpt for breath control. Use the techniques mentioned previously. i.e., practice at a faster tempo or work backwards from the end of the solo to the beginning.

Richard Wagner
Die Meistersinger von Nürnberg (1868), Prelude, mm. 27-29

Concentrate on taking a slow, deep breath for this expressive solo. Do this with a relaxed and expanded body for maximum intake.

CHAPTER 3
Embouchure

Embouchure (French, the formation of the lips) regulates and focuses the energy of the air column through the flute. The English word *pure* or the syllable *pooh* creates the same shape with the lips. In this approach to *embouchure*, roll the bottom lip slightly forward, relax the top lip rather than stretching tightly against the teeth, and place the corners firmly on the canine teeth. Concentrate on a small, round aperture (opening in the lips) with the size and shape of a broom straw or a straight pin. A flexible *embouchure* regulates the air column for smooth phrasing, breath control and register changes.

Embouchure Exercises

Harmonics prepare a flutist's *embouchure* like a singer vocalizes to warm up. Increase air speed and move lips forward without tightening the throat or forcing upper notes. Always slur harmonic exercises. Practice each harmonic series in reverse order to develop flexibility and control.

Follow these simple practice suggestions to develop the *embouchure*:

1) Set *embouchure* before the first note.

2) Maintain *embouchure* through the last note.

3) Hear the next pitch with a natural adjustment of *embouchure* for the phrase.

Harmonic Exercises

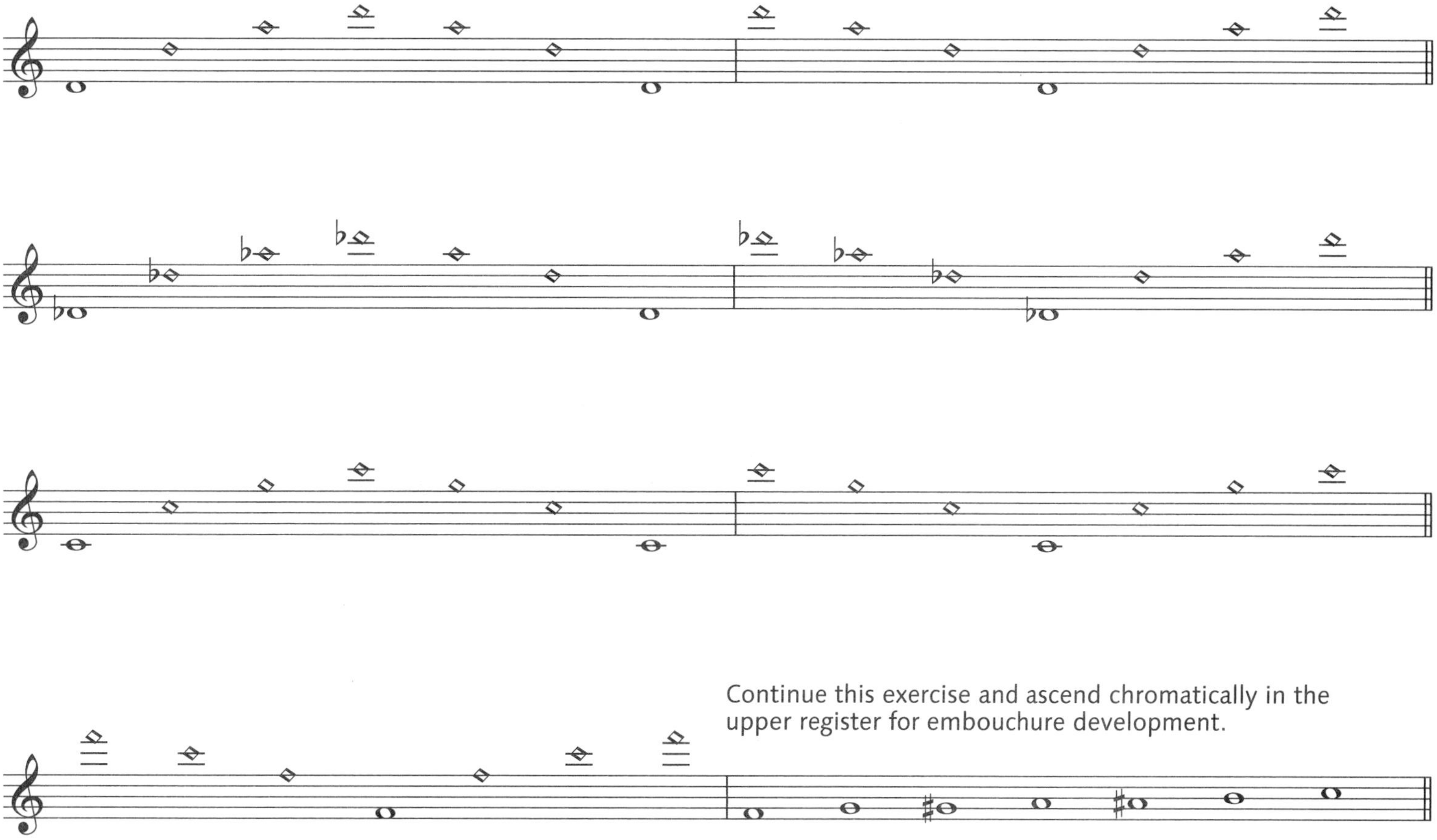

Continue this exercise and ascend chromatically in the
upper register for embouchure development.

Octave Exercises

etc.
chromatically to:
etc.
chromatically to:

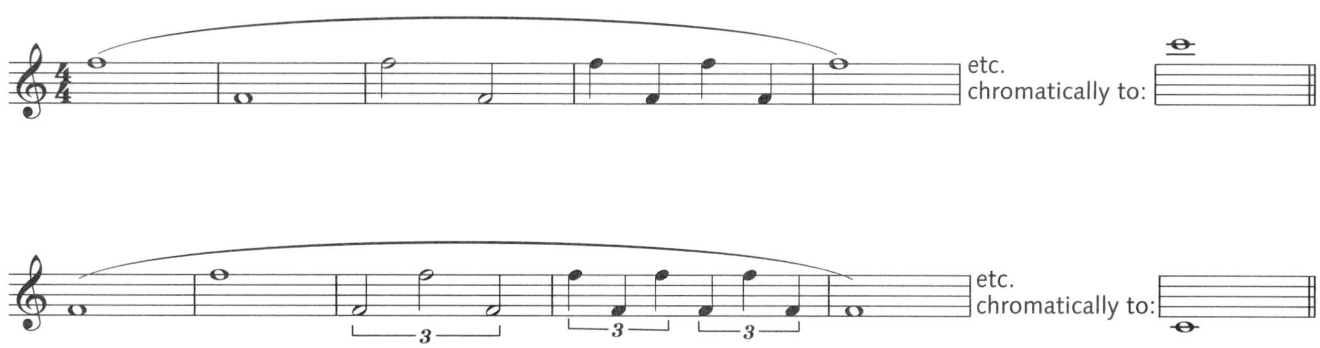

Practice ascending and descending octaves for *embouchure* flexibility.

Musical Excerpts

Georges Bizet
L'Arlésienne Suite No. 2, op. 23, movement 3, Menuet, mm. 3-30

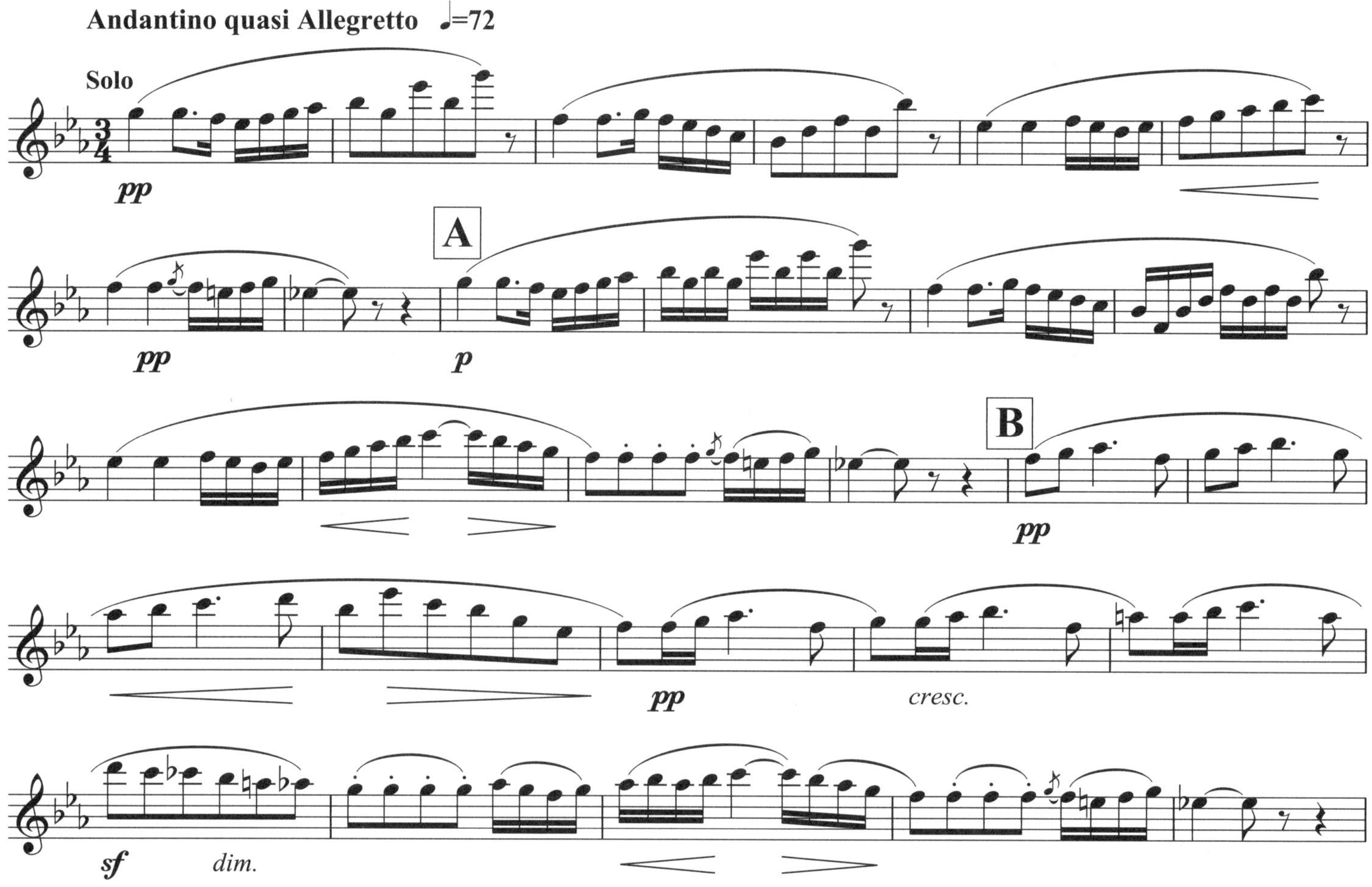

Practice harmonic exercises to develop *embouchure* flexibility needed in this beautiful excerpt. Always move eyes forward for smooth, connected phrasing.

Johannes Brahms
Symphony No. 4 in E Minor, op. 98, movement 4, mm. 89-105

Embouchure refinement determines phrase direction and projection in this famous excerpt. Octave exercises develop intonation in the difficult key of E Minor.

Ludwig van Beethoven
Symphony No. 3 in E flat Major, op. 55, movement 4, mm. 172-200

Rapid octave changes, a wide dynamic range and lack of breathing opportunities challenge *embouchure* strength and flexibility. Practice harmonics in reverse order to develop consistence and confidence at soft dynamic levels in the upper register.

CHAPTER 4
Phrasing

Music is an active art, requiring energy and flow for creation of sound. Phrasing begins with the basic building blocks of music, scales and arpeggios. Flow and direction in the air column adds color to individual pitches, and musical content follows the inherent tension and release found in scales. Hear the starting pitch with the internal ear then sing or whistle the scale with inflection, moving the eyes ahead to prepare for points of arrival in the scale. Maintain loose hands and fingers at both slow and fast tempos for smooth connections between notes. Spin the air column throughout the phrase to project and sustain the line. Tight fingers, hands and arms will create vertical phrasing, with limited dynamic range and projection, so prepare for note changes by thinking forward and moving the eyes ahead through the phrase. Rhythm brings life to music, and subdivision in longer note values maintains accuracy. Spin the air column throughout the phrase to project and sustain the line.

Phrase Exercises

Arpeggios outline the bone structure of a key, so practice the exercise with a clear sense of harmony and phrasing. Think forward to the points of arrival at the bottom and top of the arpeggio. For smooth phrase connections, avoid mechanical finger movements or bumps with the air column. Memorize and transpose the pattern in all twelve keys as an ear training exercise. Vary rhythms and dynamics for an additional challenge.

Musical Excerpts

Alexander Borodin
Prince Igor (1890) Polovetsian Dance No. 17, mm. 31-40

Spin the air column forward with direction and flow that follows the natural shape of the line. Subdivide longer notes for accurate rhythm throughout the phrases.

Richard Wagner
Tannhäuser (1845), Act II, Scene II, *Marsch. Einzug der Gäste*, mm. 1-8

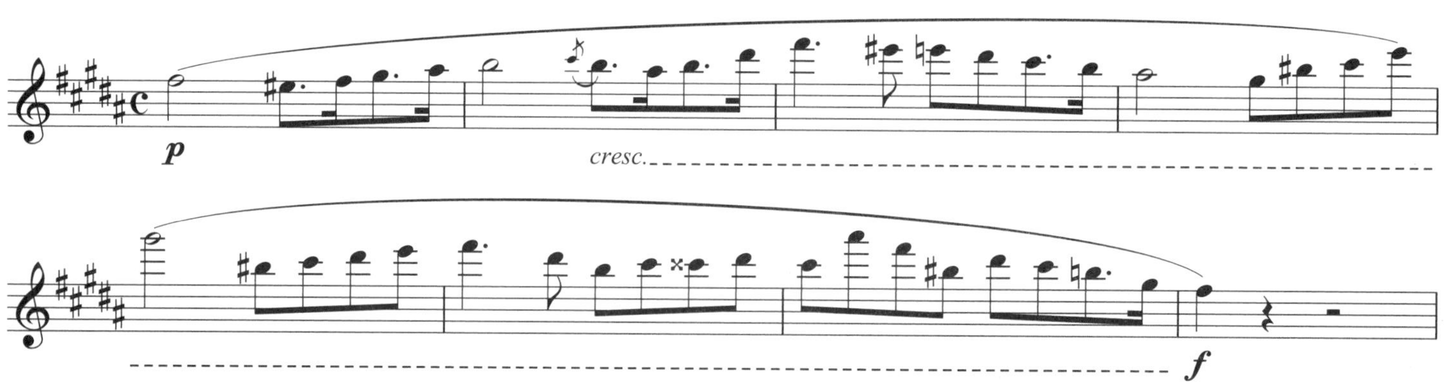

Connect the notes in a legato style carefully observing rhythmic details and dynamic markings for expressive phrasing in this elegant melody.

Felix Mendelssohn-Bartholdy
Symphony No. 4 in A Major, op. 90 (Italian), movement 2, mm. 11-35, Flutes 1 & 2

The flute parts are woven in a seamless texture. Phrase direction follows the contour of the lines. Subdivide throughout, particularly in longer notes and rests, in the style of chamber music.

Johannes Brahms
Symphony No. 1 in C Minor, op. 68, movement 4, mm. 22-26

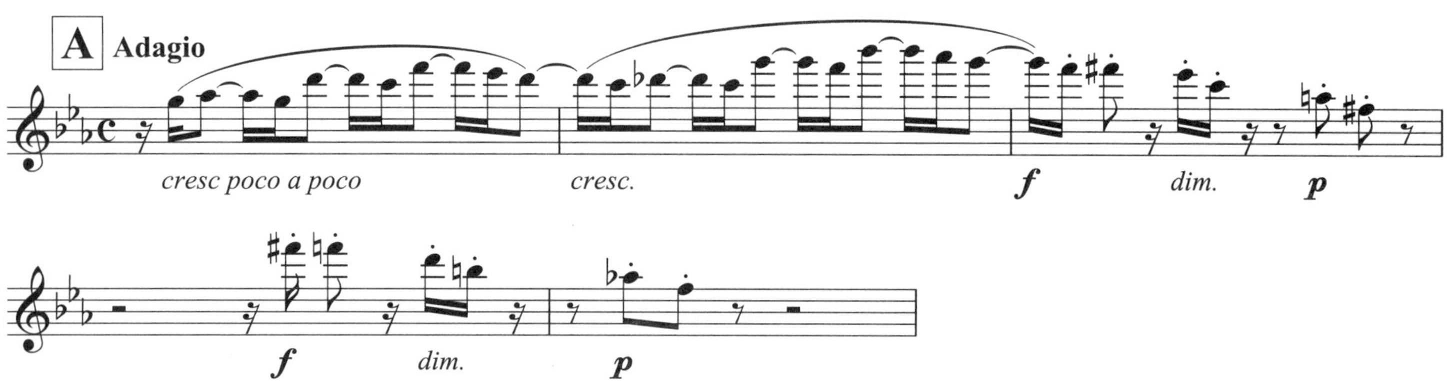

Brahms adds rhythmic complexity to this simple melody with syncopation, ties, and rests. For phrase development, fill in rests with notes, articulate ties, and subdivide longer notes.

Ludwig van Beethoven
Symphony No. 3 in E flat Major, op. 55, movement 2, *Marcia funebre*, mm. 166-180

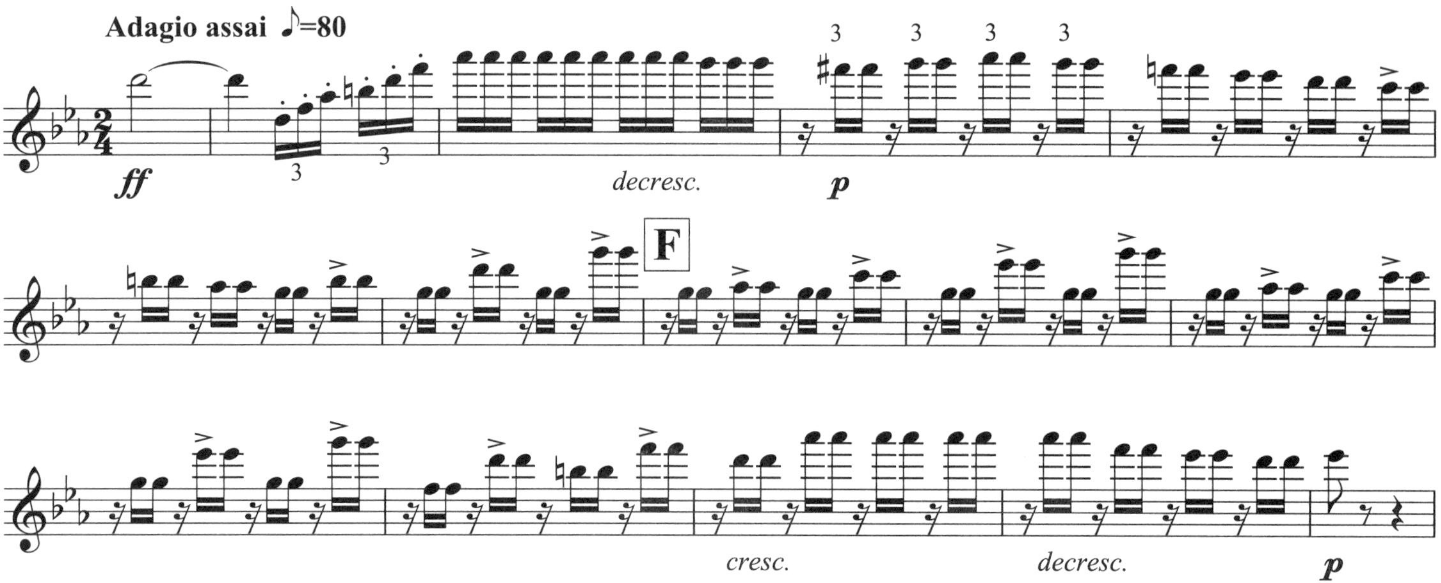

Using scale and arpeggio patterns, Beethoven builds a framework in the solo, then introduces complexity by omitting downbeats and adding syncopated accents. Practice filling in rests to develop rhythmic accuracy and phrase direction.

Pyotr Ilyich Tchaikovsky
Symphony No. 5 in E Minor, op. 64, movement 2, mm. 119-127

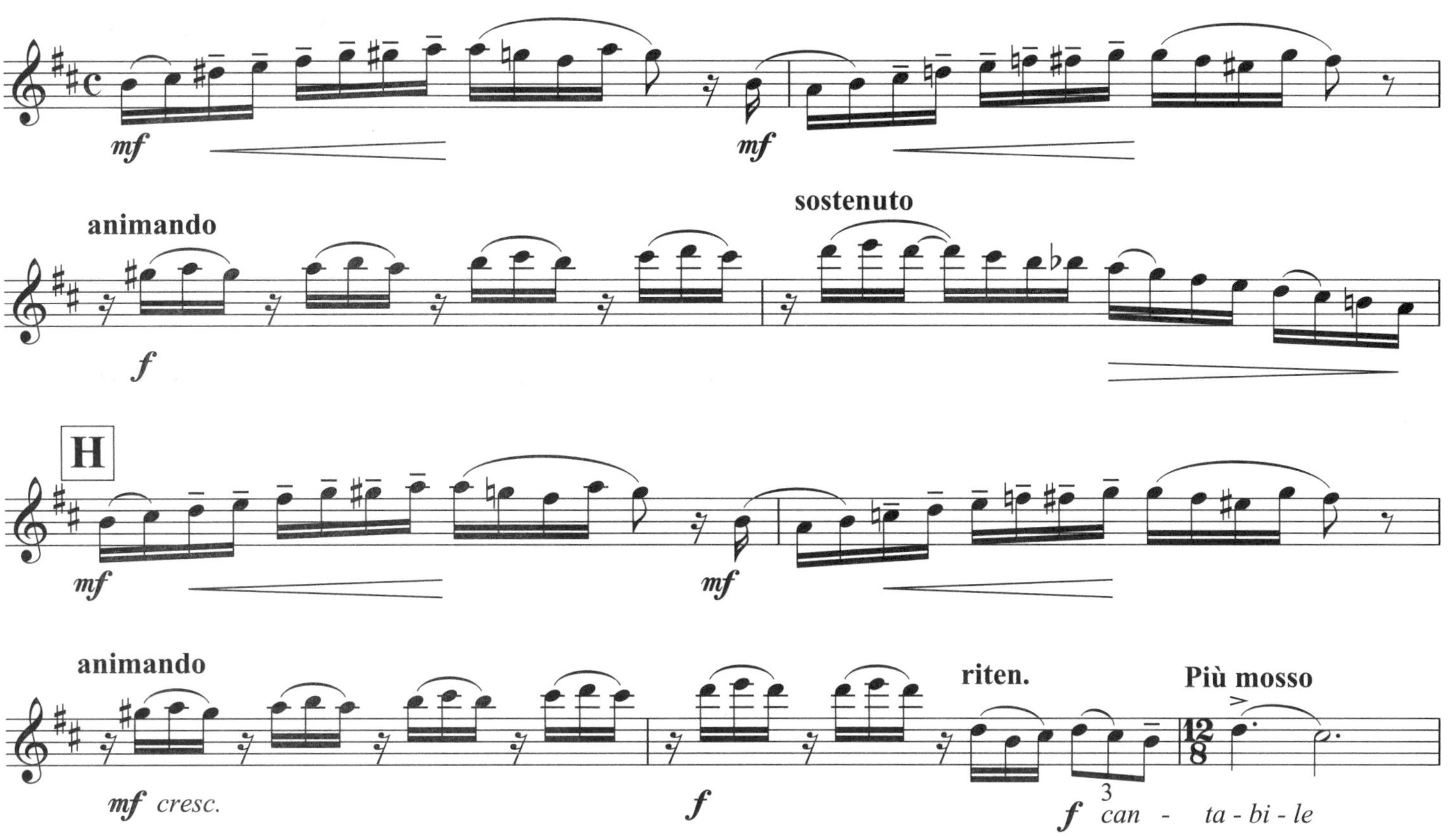

In this dramatic excerpt, practice the indicated *rubato* tempos and dynamic contrasts with exaggeration to develop intensity in phrases.

Antonín Dvorák
Symphony No. 8 in D Major, op. 88, movement 1, mm. 62-76

Think of direction and energy through the solo, with light articulation and a bouncy air column. Subdivide through trills, longer notes, and rests with the underlying eighth note pulse to add phrasing and maintain rhythmic accuracy.

Pyotr Ilyich Tchaikovsky
Symphony No. 4 in F Minor, op. 36, movement 1, mm. 35-50

Spin the air column through this long excerpt for direction, color and energy in phrasing.

CHAPTER 5
Articulation

Articulation is always light, with the tongue in a forward, relaxed position in the mouth. Release the air at the beginning of the phrase with a small tongue motion. Maintain constant air speed for phrase direction through articulate passages. Finishing or stopping notes with the tongue creates vertical phrasing, so remember to leave the sound spinning forward at the end of the phrase. For speed and endurance, use the air column to support and sustain articulation. Maintain a beautiful tone quality and resonant sound throughout articulate passages. Because the tongue is a muscle that tires easily, building endurance through daily articulation practice is essential. Use these exercises to develop speed and endurance in combination with the phrasing of the scale.

Articulation Exercises

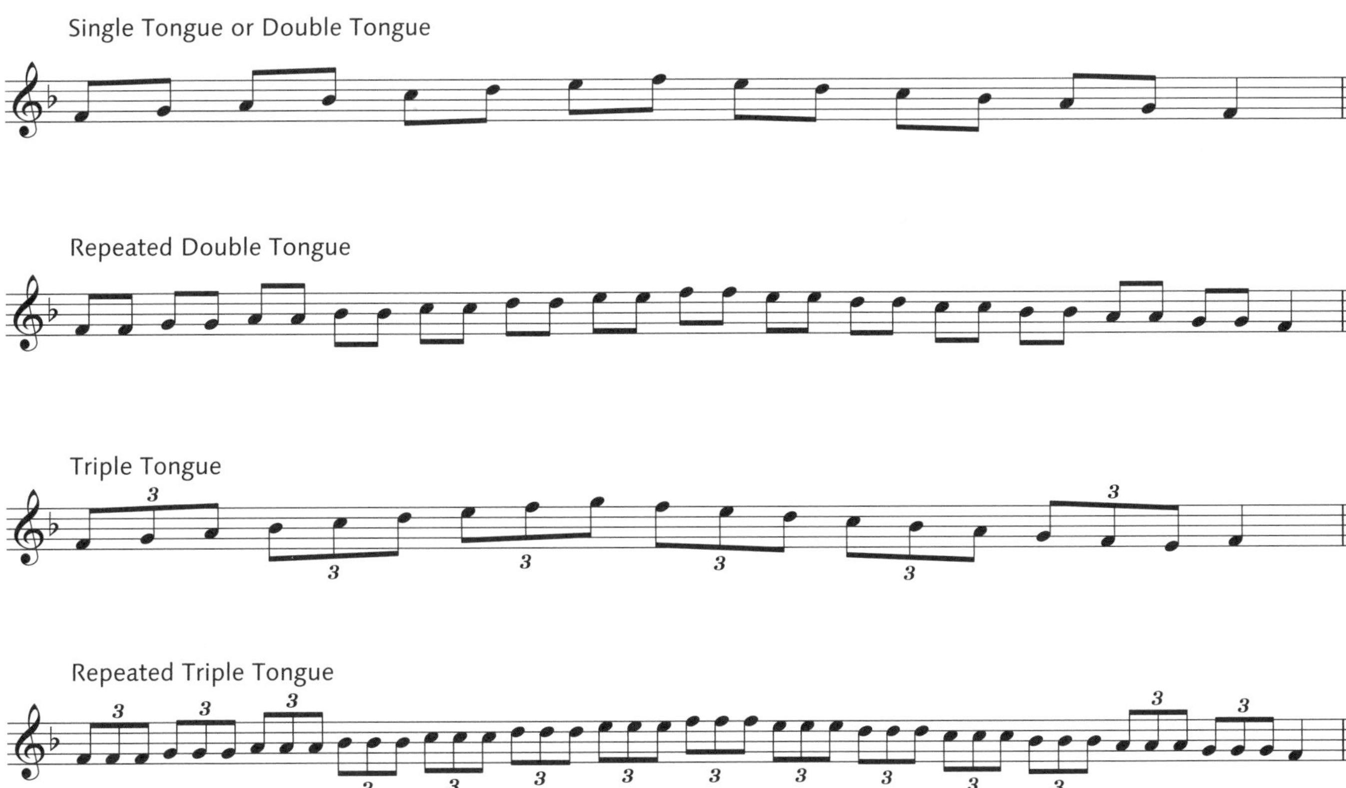

Concentrate on using an *oo* vowel or a French *u* in the scale exercises rather than focusing on the consonant sound (T or D) created by the tongue. For a singer, vowels provide musical content and phrase direction to the text. The flute responds to this approach as well. When multiple tonguing (double or triple), remember to keep the tongue forward, minimizing disturbance of the air column and sustaining phrases through articulate passages.

Chromatic scales challenge tongue and finger coordination. Be creative in practice. Memorize and transpose these simple exercises to all twelve keys. Vary rhythm patterns, articulation styles, dynamics, and register of the flute to complement the technical and musical challenges of repertoire.

Musical Excerpts

Antonín Dvorák
Symphony No. 9 in E Minor, op. 95 (From the New World), movement 1, mm. 411-418

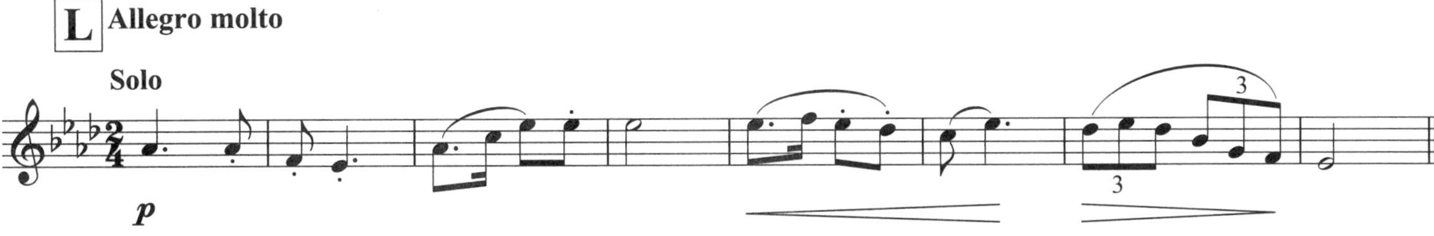

Use light articulation with energy and support behind the tongue to add color and direction. Staccato notes are spaced, maintaining energy and direction in phrasing throughout this prominent solo passage.

Nicolai Rimsky-Korsakov
Scheherazade, op. 35, movement 2, mm 424-436

Think of long phrases in this beautiful solo with light articulation on the short slurs. Sustain phrases through slur endings and longer notes for clear projection and dramatic expression.

Nicolai Rimsky-Korsakov
Scheherazade, op. 35, movement 4, mm.38-85

Vivo ♩ = ♩. = 88

a2

mf

3

3

A 16 B a2

f

A strong rhythmic pulse adds energy to this exciting excerpt. Prepare for technical challenges by moving eyes forward constantly and maintain loose fingers, hands, and arms for smooth phrasing.

Robert Schumann
Symphony No. 1 in B flat Major, op. 38 (Spring), movement 1, mm. 19-22

Use a fast, spinning air column for energy and projection in this excerpt. For practice, slur the descending chromatic scale to develop phrase connection and remember to maintain energy through the rests to the end of the passage.

Georges Bizet,
Carmen Suite No. 1, op. 74, movement 3, Seguedille (Act I), mm. 1-52

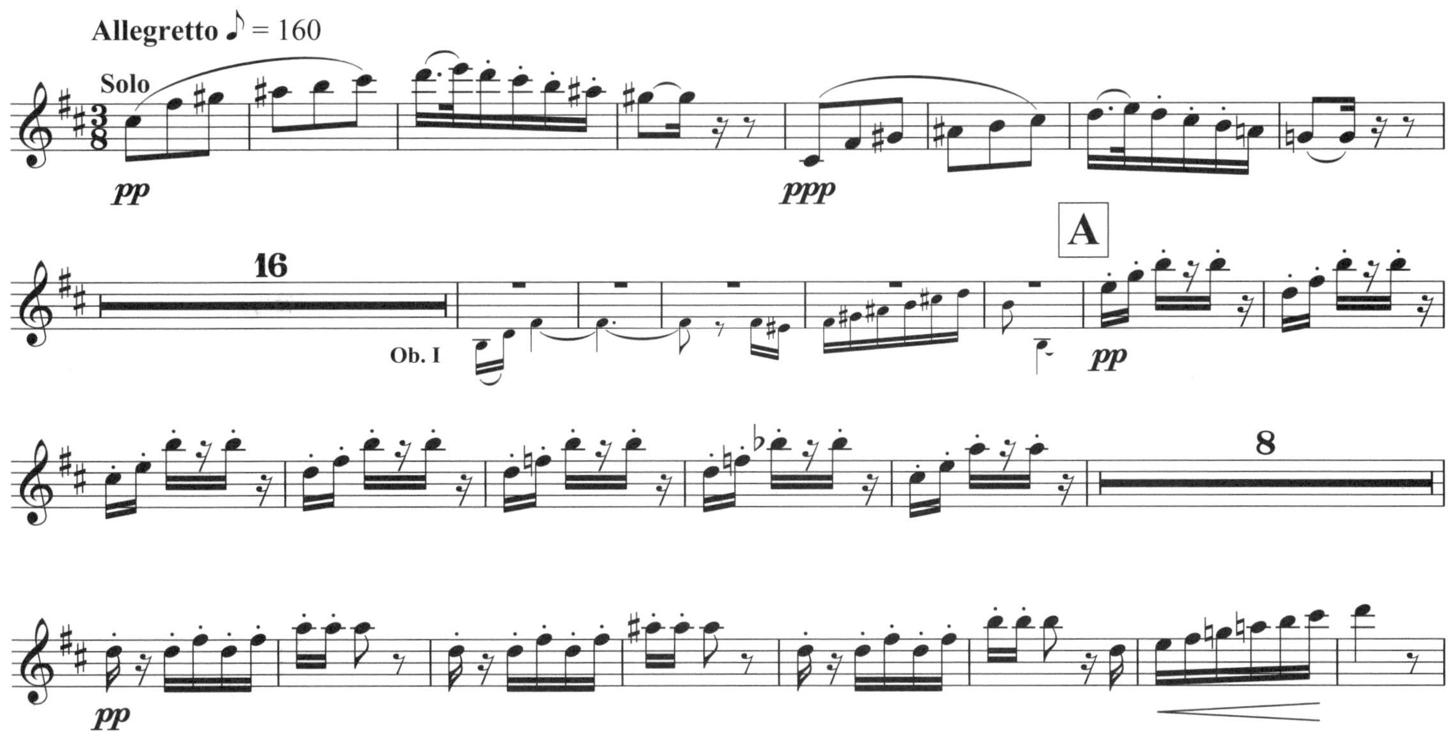

This excerpt combines legato and articulate styles. It's helpful to practice the articulate passages slurred to develop phrasing and style.

Felix Mendelssohn-Bartholdy
Incidental Music to Shakespeare's ***A Midsummer Night's Dream***, op. 61, Scherzo, mm. 37-84

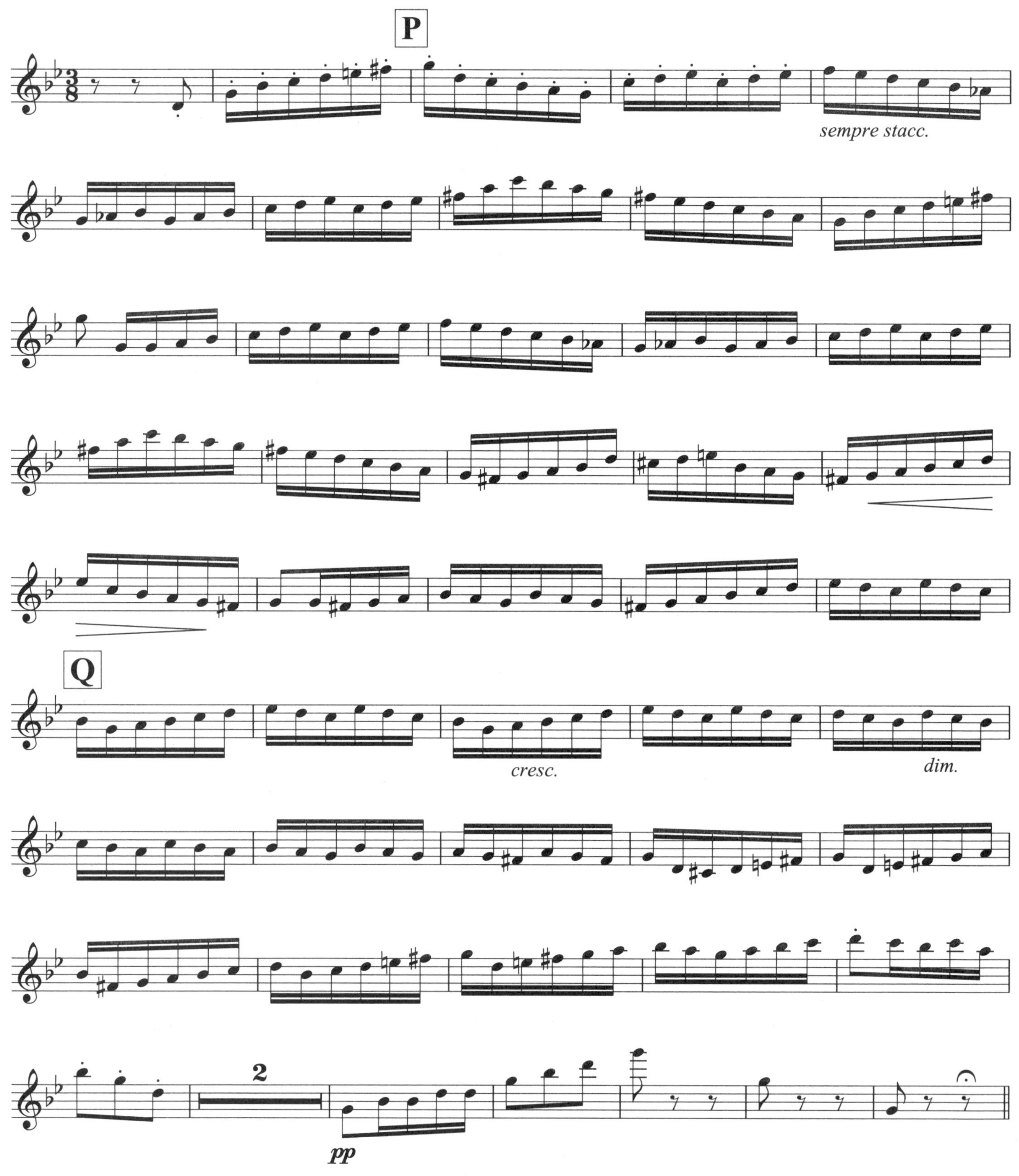

Practice this famous excerpt in a legato style before adding the challenge of articulation. Coordinate tongue and fingers precisely. Concentrate on sustaining the air column behind finger changes.

This page has been left blank to facilitate page turns.

Camille Saint-Saëns
Le Carnaval des Animaux (1886), movement 10, *Volière*, mm. 3-30

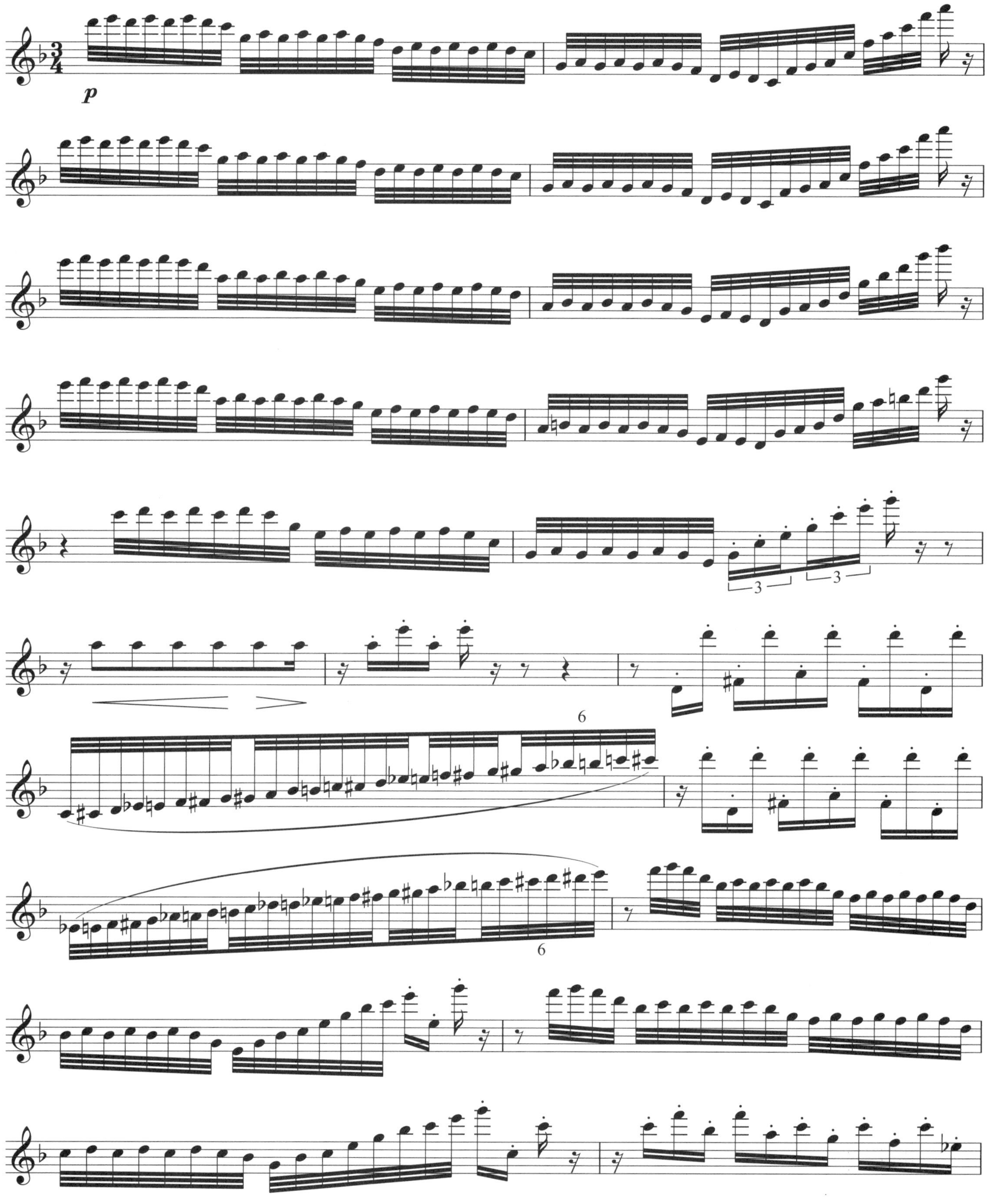

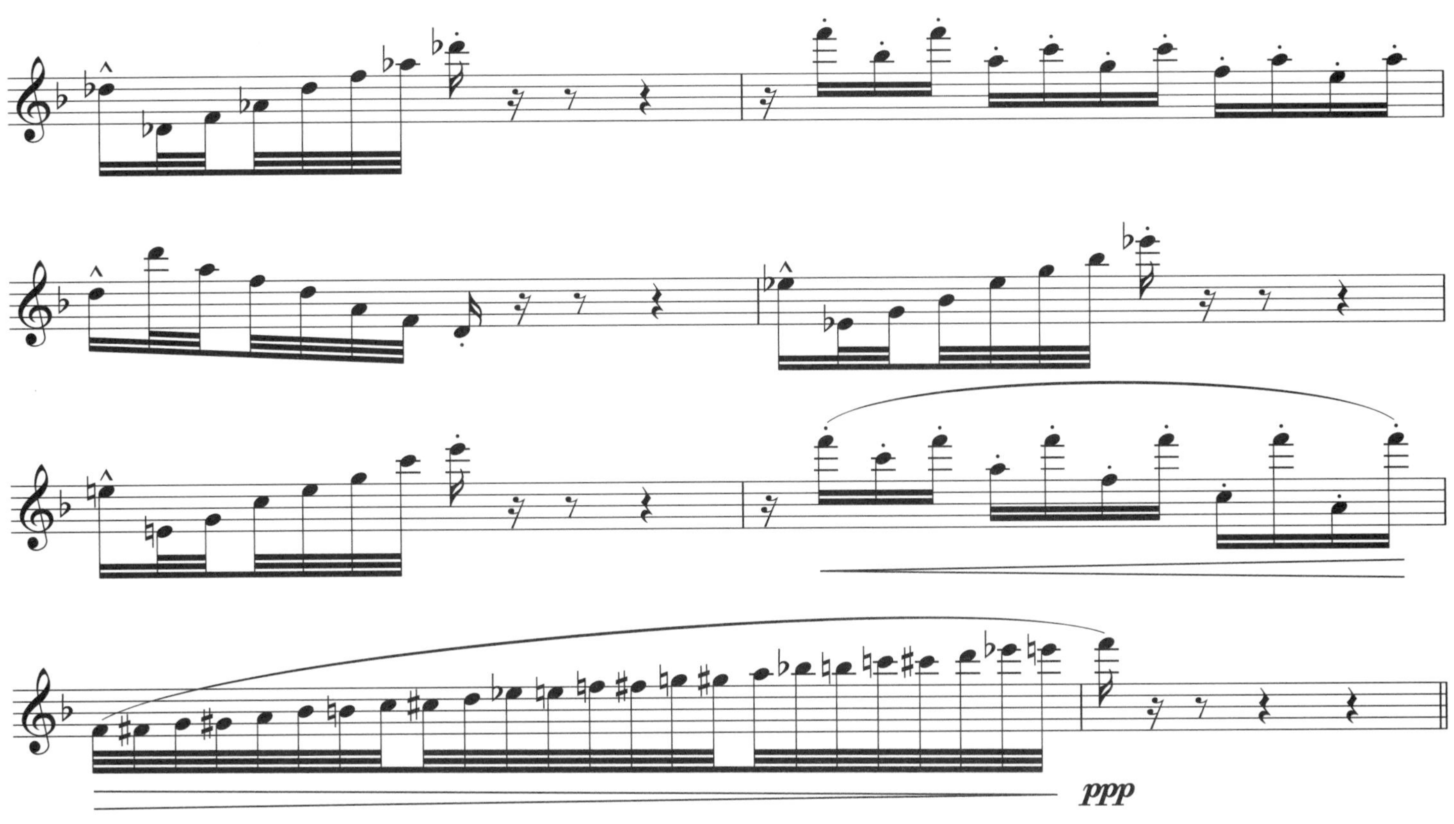

Volière (Birds) conveys the energy of a bird in flight. For speed and agility, use double tonguing throughout the excerpt. Sing through the phrases with light articulation and air support behind the tongue to maintain a beautiful, resonant tone.

CHAPTER 6
Vibrato

Vibrato is a slight alternation above and below the pitch center. As an expressive addition to tone, projection, and phrasing, vibrato adds interest and color to musical sound. After establishing a focused, consistent tone, think of vibrato like whistling, then practice daily exercises for flexibility, variety, and control in all ranges, dynamics, and styles. Use long tone studies and scales as simple exercises. Experiment with orchestral excerpts to develop artistic phrasing, color, and flow. An ideal vibrato follows the shape of the musical phrase and should never sound mechanical or structured. Avoid vibrato which is heavy, slow, and wide or shaky, fast, and narrow ("nanny-goat" vibrato or in French, *chevrotement*).

Vibrato Exercises

These exercises develop flexibility and confidence in vibrato, challenging the flutist to practice creatively by adding dynamic contrasts (forte, piano, crescendo, or decrescendo), using harmonic fingerings, and changing registers in daily exercises. Shaping vibrato speed and depth follows natural phrasing of the musical lines. After developing control in these exercises, experiment with vibrato in the following musical excerpts for added projection, musical expression and tone color.

Musical Excerpts

Johann Sebastian Bach
Sonata in B Minor, BWV 1030, movement 2, mm. 1-8

A beautiful example of Bach's style, practice this excerpt without vibrato for tone color, direction, and legato phrasing. Then add vibrato at arrival points to strengthen harmonic movement. In the style of the Baroque, vibrato should enhance rather than overpower the phrase.

Ludwig van Beethoven
Symphony No. 6 in F Major, op. 68 (The Pastoral), movement 2, mm. 57-67

Beethoven's *Pastoral Symphony* evokes scenes of tranquility. The vibrato style should be consistent with the overall mood of the music. Sing through the phrases to points of arrival and add vibrato to project and define cadence points.

Johannes Brahms
Symphony No. 1 in C Minor, op. 68, movement 2, mm. 49-51

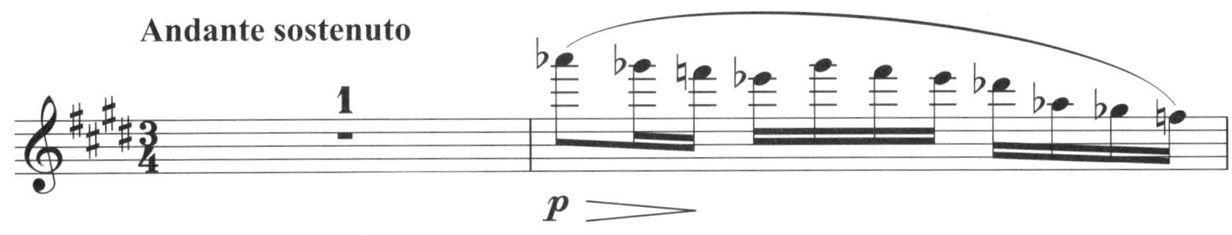

Use a singing vibrato to project the flute solo over the orchestral texture and prepare for the difficult entrance with a deep, relaxed breath in the preceding measure of rest.

CHAPTER 7
Dynamics

Dynamic contrast provides color and life in music with an infinite variety of shadings available in phrasing. A flutist combines direction, air speed, and *embouchure* flexibility for sound projection to the back of the hall. Loud dynamic levels encourage relaxation, allowing the sound to flow without restraint, while soft dynamic levels are produced by a fast air stream and small aperture in the lips. The art of projection develops with experience, so practice in locations of various sizes and acoustics to expand sound and eliminate physical habits of tension and restriction.

Dynamic Exercises

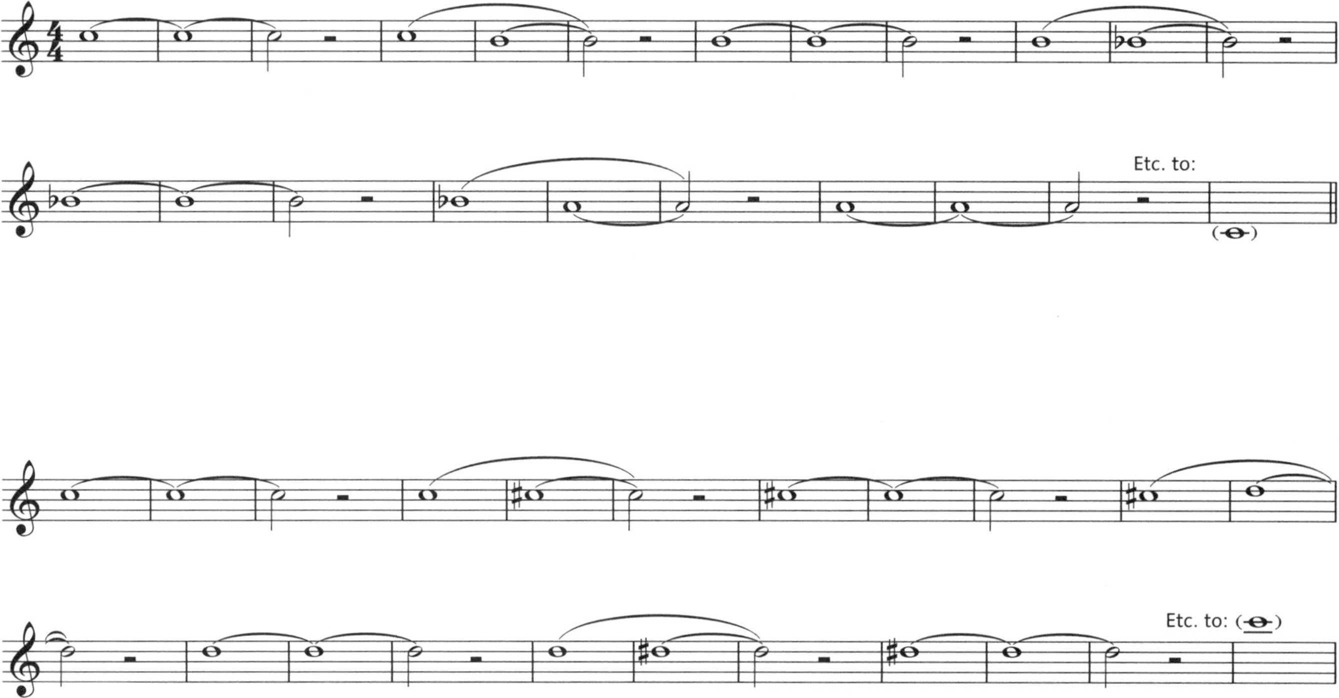

Practice long tones daily, adding color, direction, and dynamic shading throughout the exercise. Experiment in practice, adding variety in dynamics (forte, piano, crescendo, or decrescendo), rhythms (shorter or longer note values) or register (8va higher or lower) to coordinate with musical repertoire challenges.

Musical Excerpts

Nicolai Rimsky-Korsakov
Scheherazade, op. 35, movement 3, mm. 44-48

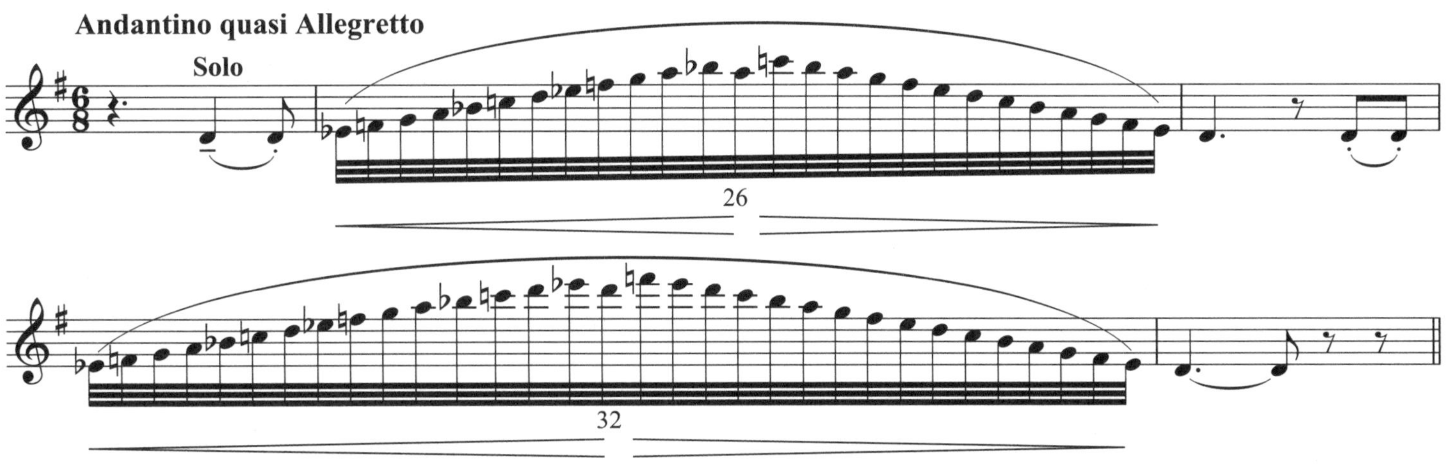

Nicolai Rimsky-Korsakov
Scheherazade, op. 35, movement 3, mm. 161-165

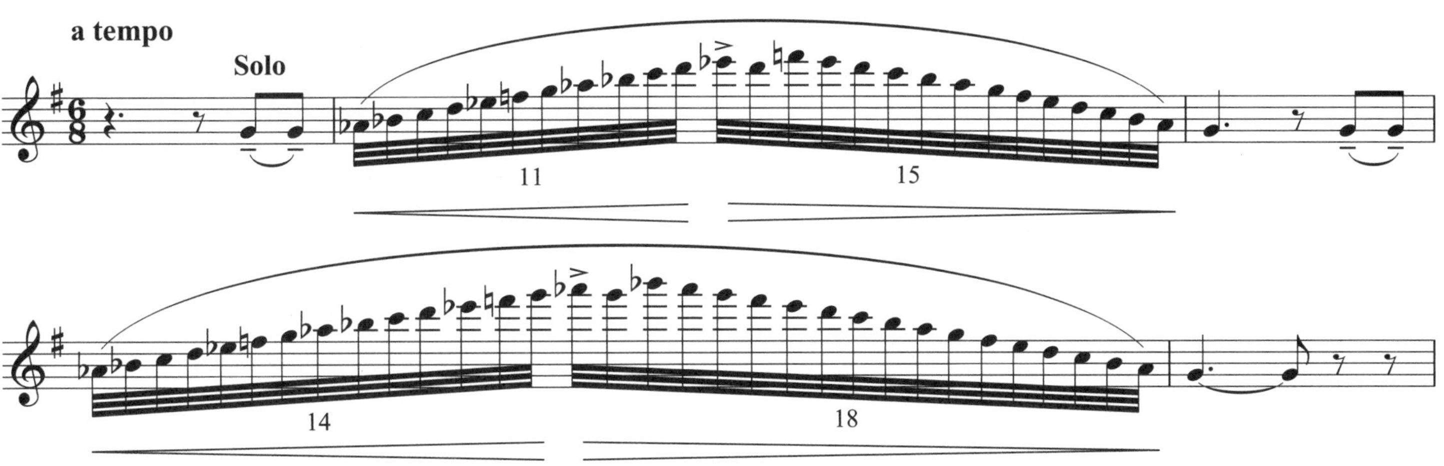

Dynamic shading follows the natural rise and fall of the scales and requires *embouchure* flexibility, air speed. Smooth finger connections to project phrasing through the solos.

Claude Debussy
Prélude à L'Après-midi d'un faune (1876), mm. 33-37

Begin the solos at a soft volume with a gradual crescendo to the marked dynamic. Exaggerate contrasts between the phrases and remember to maintain direction to the arrival point of each phrase.

Ludwig van Beethoven
Symphony No. 3 in E flat Major, op. 55, movement 2, Marcia funebre, mm. 81-89

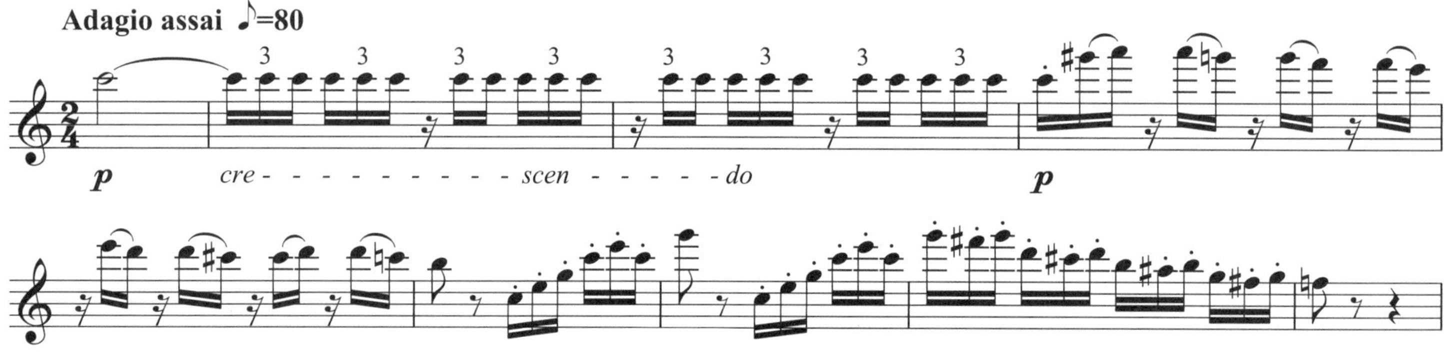

This excerpt provides practice with dynamic change over a repeated note. The underlying harmony shapes, directs, and colors the phrase. Prepare for the *subito piano* with *embouchure* flexibility to anticipate the dynamic change.

Ludwig van Beethoven
Symphony No. 7 in A Major, op. 92, movement 1, mm. 41-53

Begin this excerpt at *mf* and *diminuendo* through the ascending scale, continuing in a *piano dolce* style. To achieve Beethoven's dramatic effect, observe the written *pianissimo* for the entire measure before beginning the crescendo that builds to the end of the passage.

CHAPTER 8
Ornaments

Ornaments, including *appoggiaturas*, grace notes, mordents, trills, and turns, are musical decorations that originated as improvised additions to a melodic line. Every ornament is a simple phrase, with the underlying harmonic structure as a guide to dynamic shading and melodic direction through the ornament. Practice phrases first without ornaments to build technical confidence. Develop breath control, and determine phrase points, then add the ornaments back into the passage, maintaining the relationship of main notes to the ornamental decorations. Move the energy of the air column through the *embouchure* for smooth connections, relaxing fingers, hands, and arms to avoid a mechanical sound and solve the technical challenges of the ornament.

Ornament Exercises

Theobald Boehm
Etude in Bb Major, Op. 26/5, mm. 1-4

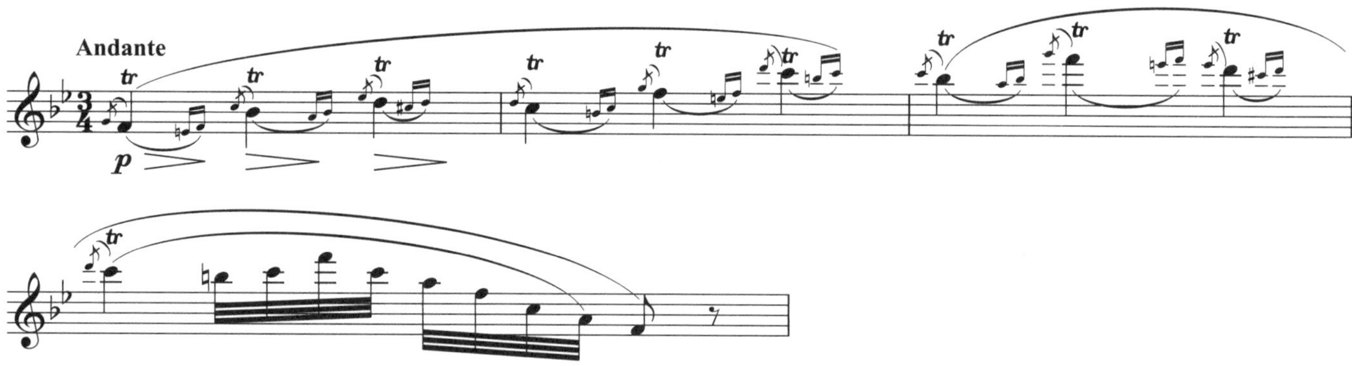

Practice first without ornaments for smooth phrasing, then practice ornaments separately to develop technical control. Transpose the phrase to all twelve keys for confidence with multiple sharps or flats, focusing on the beautiful melody for expression and projection through the ornament.

Friedrich Kuhlau
Etude in C# Minor, Divertissement Op. 68/6, mm. 1-44

Kuhlau's phrasing is expressive and dramatic with ornamentation of simple scales and arpeggios in the style of the 19th century. Connect phrases smoothly and maintain direction and flow in the air column throughout the excerpt.

Musical Excerpts

Robert Schumann
Symphony No. 1 in B flat Major, op. 38 (Spring), movement 4, mm. 176-181

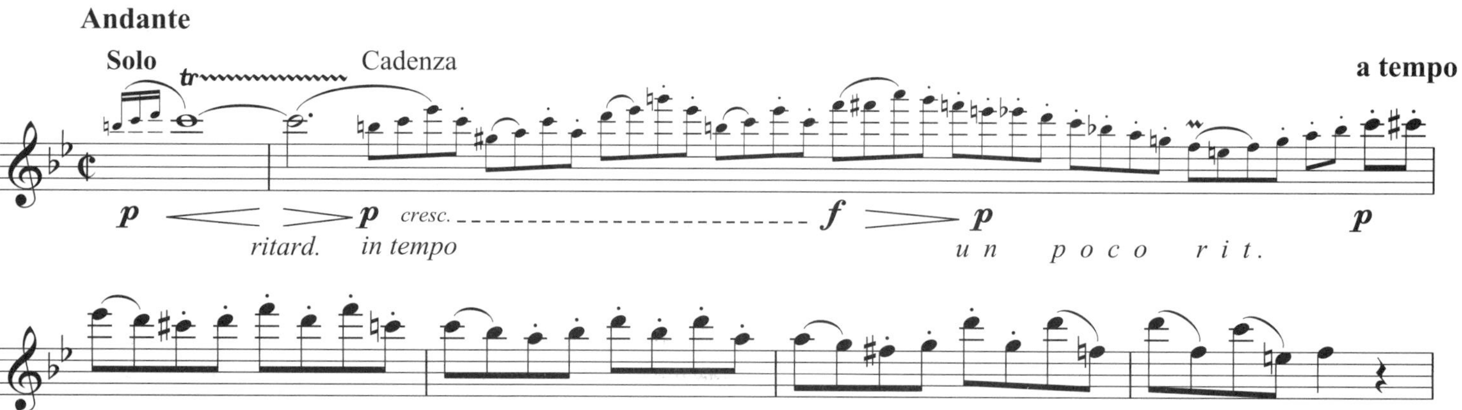

Think of improvising this cadenza, with trills, turns, and mordents to ornament the basic phrases. Be creative in practice, exaggerating dynamic contrasts and tempo changes to project the energy of spring.

Ludwig van Beethoven
Symphony No. 6 in F Major, op. 68 (The Pastoral), movement 2, mm. 129-136

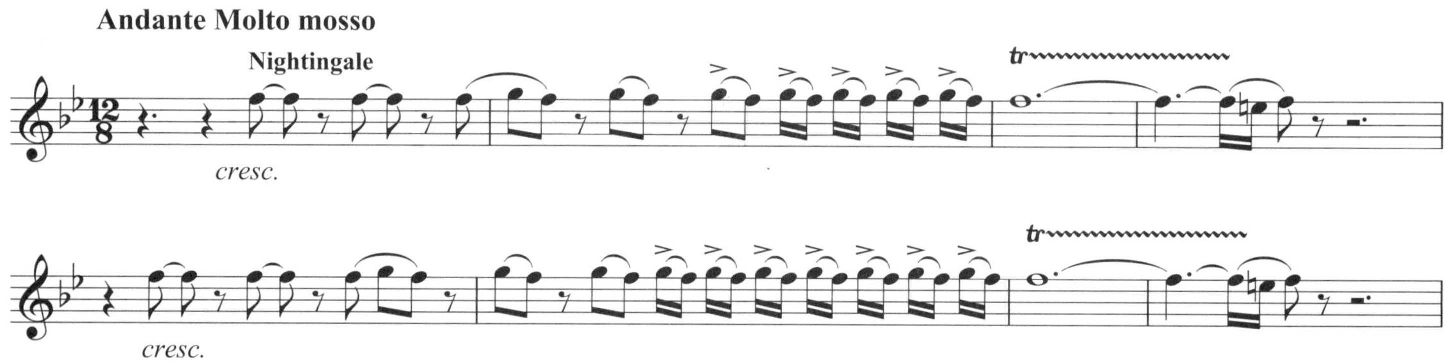

An example of written ornamentation, the Nightingale sings with energy, freedom and urgency through the phrases. Stress upper *appoggiaturas* (accented notes), releasing tension on the second note of the slurs. Shape the trills as a bird sings through the night air.

Richard Wagner
Rienzi (1842), Overture, mm. 7-8

Broadly sustain the ornamentation in this famous theme, following Wagner's direction to begin the turn with the lower neighbor (i.e. D C# D E D). As an ear training exercise, memorize and transpose the phrase to all twelve keys.

Theobald Boehm
Variations on a Theme of Nel cor più, op. 4, Introduction/Cadenza, mm. 30

This beautiful cadenza displays a range of expression, with romantic phrasing, dynamic contrast, a graceful melodic turn, and dramatic ritard at the end. Memorize and transpose the cadenza, varying tempos and dynamics in the style of the 19th century.

Richard Wagner
Die Meistersinger von Nürnberg (1868), Act III, Scene IV, mm. 1-4

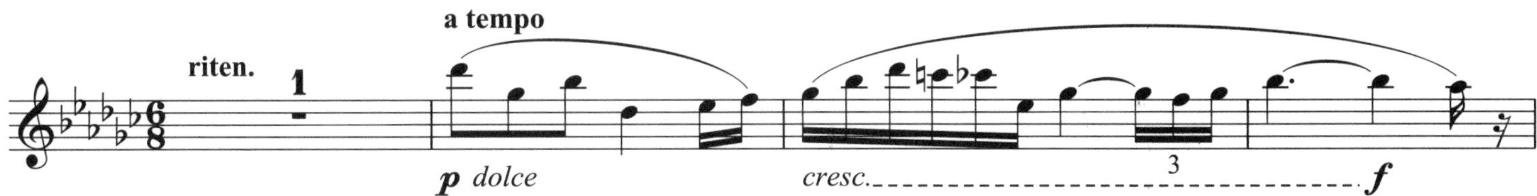

This is another example of written ornamentation, and Wagner adds the turn formula to the arrival point of the phrase. Begin the excerpt at a piano dolce dynamic, sustaining the crescendo to the end of the phrase for dramatic effect.

This page has been left blank to facilitate page turns.

CHAPTER 9
Practice

There is no substitute for slow, organized practice to develop confidence and accuracy in performance. In new repertoire, always identify the scale and arpeggio as well as key changes or modulations found within the music for improved learning efficiency and retention of new material. To improve phrasing and technical accuracy, study the music first before playing, determining the key, meter, and form. Count or tap rhythms aloud, identifying repeated patterns and sequences. Change rhythms in technical passages; and break up practice sessions to build concentration skills and avoid physical and mental fatigue. Remember to create phrasing, tone color, and musical content in practice to encourage mental activity, avoid boredom and develop the highest standards of musical artistry.

This space has been left blank to facilitate page turns.

Practice Exercises

Joachim Andersen
Etude in G Major, Op. 33/3

Before practicing this etude, identify the key and time signatures, scan the music for melodic and rhythmic patterns, and determine direction and flow of phrases. Sing the scale and arpeggio, building a framework for the patterns of Andersen's lyric etude.

Musical Excerpts

Ludwig van Beethoven
Symphony No. 4 in B flat Major, op. 60, movement 2, mm. 64-72

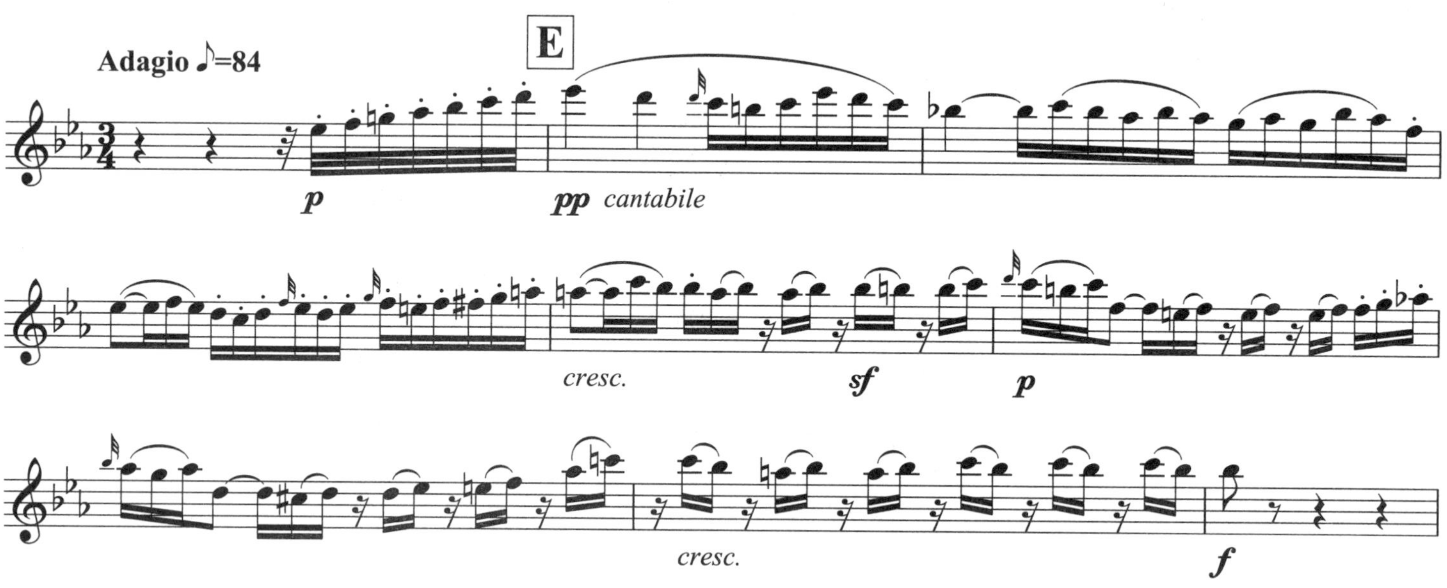

Before playing aloud, study this excerpt, identifying scales, arpeggios, rhythmic patterns, sequences, articulations, and dynamics. Listen to a recording of the Symphony with a score for reference, then practice the excerpt aloud for improved learning efficiency and retention.

Pyotr Ilyich Tchaikovsky
Symphony No. 4 in F Minor, op. 36, movement 2, mm. 85-97

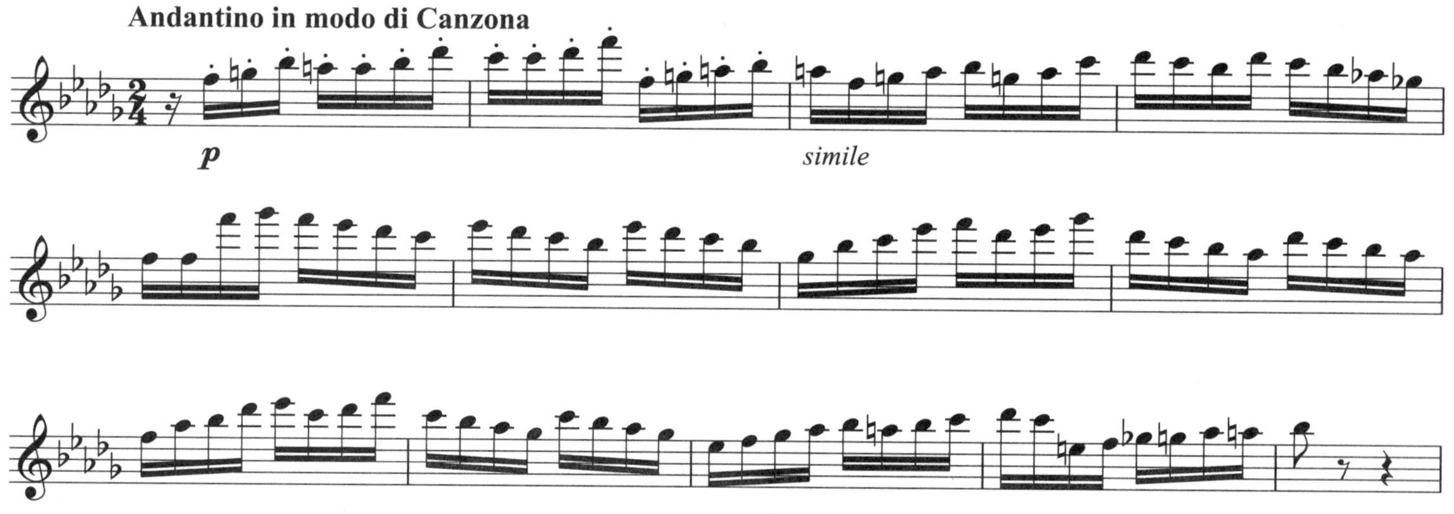

Practice the Bb minor scale and arpeggio, then study phrase patterns, hearing pitches internally and singing or whistling the music before playing aloud. Move the eyes forward through the phrase to prepare for accidentals and unexpected changes in phrase direction.

Appendix I
Musical Excerpts

Appendix II
Composer Biographies

Johann Sebastian Bach (1685 – 1750)
Born into a musical family and orphaned at age ten, as a boy J. S. Bach lived with his elder brother, Johann Christophe, an organist in the town of Ohrduhf. Learning the skills of organ repair and tuning from his brother, Bach's first paid position as a musician was in Weimar, and in 1708, he was appointed organist and chamber musician at the court of Saxe-Weimar. Hired by Prince Leopold as Kapellmeister at Cöthen in 1717, the prince's love of music inspired many of Bach's greatest works, including the *Brandenburg Concerti*; cello and orchestral suites; and sonatas and partitas for solo violin and flute. Appointed Kantor at Leipzig's Thomaskirche, Bach's remaining years were spent writing music for the church, including the *Mass in B Minor*; the *St. Matthew* and *St. John Passions*; and the *Magnificat in D*. A leading figure of the Baroque, Bach was a virtuoso organist, harpsichordist, violinist, and master of the fugue; but his greatest contribution was as the composer of over a thousand works, and his death in 1750 has been denoted by historians as the end of the Baroque era.

Ludwig van Beethoven (1770 – 1827)
The son of a court musician, Beethoven was born in Bonn, Germany, and moved to Vienna in his early twenties, where he studied composition with Franz Joseph Haydn and established a reputation as a virtuoso pianist. His work is divided into three periods (Early, Middle and Late), and the Early period reflects the classical style of Mozart and Haydn. Breaking with tradition, Beethoven rejected the idea of patronage and supported himself by commissions, performances, teaching and the sale of his works. Attracted to the ideals of the Enlightenment, Beethoven was a pivotal figure in the transition from the Classic to the Romantic periods, and his temperament reflected the passionate emotions of the 19th century artist. Despite a loss of hearing, he continued working through the Middle and Late periods of his life, and his compositions include nine symphonies, nine concerti, the opera *Fidelio*, 32 piano sonatas, 16 string quartets, the *Missa Solemnis*, and various chamber works. Beethoven died in March of 1827, and a crowd of 20,000 Viennese followed his coffin to the Währing Cemetery west of Vienna.

Georges Bizet (1838 – 1875)
Born in 1838 in Paris, Bizet was a precocious child, and by age four, he could read and write music. Entering the Paris Conservatoire in 1848, he received prizes in theory, piano, organ, and composition, and in 1857, he won a Prix de Rome prize for the operetta *Le Docteur Miracle*. With little success in his personal and professional life, Bizet is best known for the opera *Carmen*, although the premiere was strongly criticized for the realism of its subject matter and its dramatic staging. Now regarded as one of the finest examples of 19th century Romantic opera, Bizet never recovered from the critical response to *Carmen*. He died in 1875 at the age of thirty-six. Bizet was a master of melody, counterpoint, and instrumental color, and his works include the *Symphony in C*, written when he was a student at the Paris Conservatoire; *L'Arlesienne Suites I and II*; two additional operas, *Les Pêcheurs de Perles* and *La jolie fille de Perth*; and *Jeux d'enfants* for piano duet.

Theobald Boehm (1794 – 1881)
The son of a goldsmith, Boehm was born in 1794 in Munich, Germany, and by age eighteen was performing as an orchestral flutist. Boehm studied acoustics at the University of Munich, and in 1832 he began to experiment with flute construction and design. His multi-faceted career included Principal Flutist in the Royal Bavarian Orchestra, soloist, composer, and inventor, and he is credited with development of the modern flute still in use today. Improvements included a new fingering system; experimentation with materials such as wood, silver, and gold; and acoustical research which produced a more accurate scale. As a composer, Boehm's music was in the tradition of 19th century romanticism, with several volumes of etudes and theme and variations to his credit. After a long and successful career, he died in Munich in 1881.

Alexander Borodin (1833 – 1887)
Born in 1833 in St. Petersburg, Russia, Borodin studied piano as a child, but he completed a Doctorate in Medicine and earned his living as a chemist, working in both Heidelberg, Germany, and Pisa, Italy. As a member of "The Five," his style, with strong lyricism and rich harmonies, has a distinctly Russian flavor, but because he was not as prolific as his contemporaries, Borodin described himself as a "Sunday Composer." Best known for the opera *Prince Igor*, which includes the popular *Polovetsian Dances*, Borodin completed two symphonies, with a third symphony incomplete at the time of his death; two string quartets; and various chamber works.

Johannes Brahms (1833 – 1897)
A native of Hamburg, Germany, Brahms studied piano and violin with his father, an innkeeper and string bass player. In 1853, Brahms toured with the Hungarian violinist Remenyi, and during the tour he met other notable musicians of the day, including the violinist Joseph Joachim and the pianist Franz Liszt. Appointed Director of Court Concerts for the Prince of Lippe-Detmold, he combined this post with other concerts and conducting throughout Germany, developing friendships along the way with Robert and Clara Schumann, Richard Wagner, and the poet Gottfried Keller. Hired as conductor of the Gesellschaft der Musikfreunde in 1868, Brahms settled in Vienna, and the success of *German Requiem* (1869) and *Variations on a Theme of Haydn* (1873) established his reputation as a composer. Following the success and critical acclaim of his first symphony in 1876, Brahms completed three additional symphonies in his lifetime, all of which are standards of the orchestral repertoire. Praised as the successor to Beethoven and for a distinctive musical voice, his neoclassical approach combines German harmonic language with forms of the Baroque and Classical period.

Claude Debussy (1862 – 1918)
Born in St. Germain-en-Laye, France, in 1862, Debussy studied piano and composition at the Paris Conservatoire, and after winning consecutive Prix de Rome prizes in 1883 and 1884, continued his studies at Villa de Medici in Rome. His fascination for music drama, particularly Wagner's *Parsifal* and *Tristan und Isolde* prompted visits to Bayreuth to attend Wagner festivals. Known as the creator of Impressionism in music, Debussy's first significant orchestral work was *Prélude a L'après midi d'un faune* in 1894, based on the poet Stéphane Mallarmé's work of the same name. Other significant works include *Nocturne*, *La Mer*, *Image*, *Jeux*, *Pélléas et Mélisande*, *Preludes* for piano, and various chamber works. With his floating harmonies, fluid rhythms, whole tone and modal scales, Debussy's colorful orchestration, melody and texture established the musical mood of the 20th century and influenced composers from Ravel to Stravinsky to Hindemith. A rapid deterioration of health and difficult conditions during World War I led to his death in 1918 during the German bombing of Paris.

Antonin Dvorak (1841 – 1904)
Born in Bohemia in 1841, Dvorak's musical talent was recognized by his parents, and he was given the opportunity to study violin and viola. He worked as a member of the Bohemian Provisional Theater early in his career but left the orchestra to devote more time to composition. His growing reputation as a composer came to the attention of Johannes Brahms, who recommended Dvorak's music to the publisher Simrock, and a commission soon followed for the *Slavonic Dances*. He received invitations to visit England and the United States, and during a residency in New York, the famous *Ninth Symphony "From the New World"* was written. Homesick for Bohemia, Dvorak left New York in 1895 and spent his last years composing and working as director of the Prague Conservatory. His works include opera, symphonies, choral and chamber music, with many compositions unfinished at his death in 1904.

Christoph Willibald Gluck (1714 – 1787)
A native of Erasbach, Germany, Gluck was born in 1714, and after studying music and philosophy at Prague University, he travelled to Vienna and Italy under the patronage of Prince Lobkowitz. A favorable marriage secured his position at the Viennese Imperial court, and Gluck was appointed Kapellmeister to the Court Theatre by Empress Maria Thereasa in 1754. He was employed there until moving to Paris in 1773. Known for his efforts to reform opera, Gluck's style included dramatic integrity over virtuosic vocal displays, focusing on musical flow and limiting recitatives that stopped dramatic action in operas of the day. Under the patronage of Queen Marie Antoinette, Gluck wrote *Iphigénie en Aulide* in the new style, and his lasting influence is seen in the works of Mozart and the music dramas of Richard Wagner. His most famous opera is *Orfeo et Euridice*, which contains the beautiful *Menuet* and *Dance of the Blessed Spirits*. Gluck died in 1787, with 35 operas, several ballets and instrumental works to his credit.

Felix Mendelssohn-Bartholdy (1809 – 1847)
Born in 1809 into a prominent Jewish family in Hamburg, Germany, Felix moved with his family to Berlin after converting to Christianity. As a child prodigy, Mendelssohn studied violin and piano, and by age thirteen, he had already composed symphonies, concertos and other sophisticated works of quality. He performed as a pianist, organist, and conductor throughout Germany, and the popularity of his music in England led to regular performances for Queen Victoria. At age twenty he organized and conducted a concert of Bach's *St. Matthew Passion* in a first performance since the composer's death, and this renewed interest in the music of Bach enhanced his reputation in the musical world. Hired as conductor of the Leipzig Gewandhaus Orchestra at twenty-six, Mendelssohn founded the Leipzig Conservatory at age thirty-three; but a constant travel and work schedule led to exhaustion and poor health, and he died at age thirty-eight. Mendelssohn's style and character were different than the stereotypical artist of the 19th century, and his music is filled with energy, light, and color, in contrast to the dramatic, passionate extremes found in the music of his contemporaries. Mendelssohn is best known for his four symphonies, concert overtures, concerti, choral works, and chamber music, and his music is performed regularly in concert and recital today.

Nikolai Rimsky-Korsakov (1844 – 1908)
Born near St. Petersburg, Russia, into an aristocratic family, Nicolai began piano at age 6, but he followed the family tradition of military service and entered the Russian Navy in 1856. Maintaining his love of music, Rimsky-Korsakov alternated naval duty with periods of composition, and in 1871 he joined the faculty of St. Petersburg Conservatory as a professor of harmony and orchestration. Self taught in the methods of Western composition, Rimsky Korsakov blended elements of folk music and programmatic themes with his skill as an orchestrator, and he was a member of the Russian group of composers known as "The Five", together with Mily Balakirev, Alexander Borodin, César Cui, and Modest Mussorgsky. Known for his symphonic works, including *Capriccio Espagnol*, *Scheherazade*, and *Russian Easter Overture*, Rimsky Korsakov's unique style and skill as an orchestrator influenced a generation of Russian composers, including his students Stravinsky and Prokofiev, as well as Debussy, Ravel, and Respighi.

Gioachino Rossini (1792 – 1868)
Born into a family of Italian musicians, Rossini studied harpsichord at a young age and apprenticed to a blacksmith when his father was imprisoned for support of the Emperor Napoleon's troops. Composing his first opera at age 12 or 13, Rossini was known as "The Italian Mozart" for a melodic style reminiscent of Mozart. He traveled to the European capitals of Vienna, London and Paris to direct his operas, among them, *The Barber of Seville* (1816), his most famous, and *Guillaume Tell* (1829), his last. With 39 operas to his credit, Rossini retired from composing at the age of 38 and settled in Paris, devoting the remainder of his long life to enjoying good food and maintaining a center for artistic society in his home.

Camille Saint-Saëns (1835 – 1921)
Born in Paris, Saint-Saëns studied piano as a child, and his precocious talent as a pianist and composer was compared to the young Mozart. Entering the Paris Conservatoire at 13, Saint-Saëns won many prizes and established a reputation that led to close friendships with Franz Liszt and Hector Berlioz. He was hired as organist at the Madeleine Church in Paris and professor at the École Niedermeyer, where Fauré was one of his students. In addition to these appointments, Saint-Saëns organized concerts of the music of Liszt, Bach and Handel and was a founder of the Société National de Musique for the promotion of new French music. A prolific composer, Saint-Saëns's works include symphonies and operas, and he was the first composer to write music for the new art form of the cinema. *Le Carnival des Animaux* premiered in 1886, but because of its humorous, light-hearted style, Saint-Saëns forbade performance of the entire work, allowing only *Le Cygne* to be published in his lifetime. A prolific writer on subjects as diverse as science, history and music, he traveled throughout Europe, North Africa, and South America, and following his death in Algiers, Saint-Saens's body was returned to Paris for a state funeral and burial.

Robert Schumann (1810 – 1856)
A German Romantic composer, Schumann was born in Zwicken, Saxony, and studied piano at an early age. Since his father was a publisher and book seller, Robert developed a love for literature; however, after his father's death, musical study was no longer encouraged, and he began the study of law. A concert by the famous violinist Paganini inspired his love of music, and he returned to study piano with his old master, Friedrich Wieke. A serious hand injury prevented Schumann from pursuing a piano career, and he turned his energies instead to composition. He wrote symphonies, lieder, opera, choral music, and chamber works, but he is best known for his piano pieces, including *Papillons* and *Carnaval*, with numerous literary associations and programmatic elements. Schumann was also a respected music critic and writer, and he founded *Neue Zeitschrift für Music*, a music magazine still in publication today. A deteriorating mental condition and an attempt at suicide led Schumann to commit himself to an asylum where he died two years later.

Pyotr Ilyich Tchaikovsky (1840 – 1893)

Born in the small Russian town of Votkinsk, Tchaikovsky began piano lessons at age four, but at his family's insistence, he prepared for a career in the civil service and attended St. Petersburg's School of Jurisprudence. Following graduation, he was employed as a civil servant, but he also enrolled at the new St. Petersburg Conservatory, studying Western techniques of composition. This formal training led to conflict with "The Five," who promoted a Russian nationalistic style. His first masterpiece was the symphonic poem, *Romeo and Juliet*. Filled with emotional intensity and passion, Tchaikovsky's most popular works include six symphonies; *Swan Lake* and *The Nutcracker* ballets; piano and violin concerti; chamber music; and the opera *Eugene Onegin*. He died in St. Petersburg in November, 1893, nine days after the premiere of his *Sixth Symphony, "The Pathetique"*.

Richard Wagner (1813 – 1883)

Born in Leipzig, Germany, Wagner was the last of nine children, and his father died within six months of his birth. Raised by his mother and stepfather (an actor and playwright), he was involved in the theatre from an early age, and a performance of Weber's opera *Der Freischutz* prompted Wagner to ask his family for music lessons. Interested in both music and playwriting, the dramatic works of Shakespeare and Goethe and the musical impact of Beethoven's Symphonies inspired him to develop the "Music Drama," uniting the elements of music and drama into a new opera form. Wagner's wrote fourteen operas, including a monumental four-opera cycle, *Der Ring des Nibelungen* (1876), and his highly contrapuntal, chromatic style was a distinctive influence on musical development through the late 19th and 20th centuries.

Appendix III
Glossary of Terms

A

Adagio (It.) – A slow tempo.
Alcuna licenza (It.) – Some freedom.
Allegretto (It.) – A lively tempo but slower than Allegro.
Andante (It.) – A walking tempo.
Andantino (It.) – A tempo slightly faster than Andante.
Anima (It.) – Soul or spirit.
Animato (It.) – Lively with animation.
Assai (It.) – Very, extremely.

B

Ben (It.) – Well.

C

Cadenza (It.) – A written or improvised virtuosic passage at the cadence.
Cantabile (It.) – In a singing style.
Canzona (It.) – A song.
Con (It.) - With.
Crescendo (It.) – Increasing in volume.

D

Decrescendo (It.) – Decreasing in volume.
Di (It.) – By or with.
Diminuendo (It.) – Decreasing in volume.
Dolce (It.) – Sweetly.
Dolcissimo (It.) – As sweetly as possible.
Doux (Fr.) – Sweetly.

E

E (It.) – And.
Einzug der Gäste (Gm.) – *Arrival of the Guests.*
Espressivo (It.) – Expressive.
Et (Fr.) – And.
Expressif (Fr.) – Expressive.

F

Fermata (It.) – An indication to hold the note or rest slightly longer than its given value.
Flauto (It.) – Flute.
Flöte (Gm.) – Flute.
Forte [*f*] (It.) - Loud.
Fortissimo [*ff*] (It.) – Louder.
Fortississimo [*fff*] (It.) - Loudest.

G

Grosse flöte (Gm.) – The standard flute, with piccolo designated as kleine flöte.

I

In (It.) - In.

L

Largamente (It.) – Slowly and broadly.
Largo (It.) – Slow and broad.
Licenza (It.) – Freedom.
Lunga (It.) – Long.

M

Ma (It.) – But.
Maestoso (It.) – Majestic.
Maggiore (It.) – Major.
Marcato (It.) – Marked and with emphasis.
Marsch (Gm.) – March.
Meno (It.) – Less.
Minore (It.) – Minor.
Moderato (It.) – Moderate.
Modéré (Fr.) – Moderate.
Modo (It.) – Mode or style.
Morendo (It.) – Dying away.
Mosso (It.) – Moving.
Moto (It.) – Motion.
Movimento (It.) – Movement or tempo.

N

Non (It.) – Not.

O

Ornaments
- Appoggiatura (It.) – 𝆕
- Grace Note – 𝆔
- Mordent (It.) – 𝆝 (Upper), 𝆞 (Lower)
- Trill (It.) – *tr* or ∿∿∿
- Turn (Eng.) – ∽

P

Piano [*p*] (It.) – Soft.
Pianissimo [*pp*] (It.) – Softer.
Pianississimo [*ppp*] (It.) – Softest.
Pastorale (It.) – Pastoral and rustic.
Pesante (It.) – Heavy.
Più (It.) – More
Poco a poco (It.) – Little by little.
Prélude (Fr.) – An introduction

Q

Quasi (It.) – In the manner of.

R

Ritardando (It.) – Slowing down or holding back.

S

Scherzo (It.) – A musical joke.
Seguedille (Fr.) – A dance in $\frac{3}{4}$ time.
Sempre (It.) – Always.
Sforzando [*Sf*, *Sfp*] (It.) – A sudden, strong accent.
Simile (It.) – Continue in the same manner, i.e. articulation, tempo or style marking.
Solo (It.) – Performed by one instrument.
Sostenuto (It.) – Sustained.
Staccato (It.) – Detached or separated.
Stringendo (It.) – Pushing the tempo forward.
Symphonie, Symphony (Fr., Gm.) – A multi-movement work for orchestra.
Szene (Gm.) – Scene.

T

Tempo (It.) – Speed of the music.
Très (Fr.) – Very.
Troppo (It.) – Too much.

U

Un (Fr.) - A.

V

Valse, Waltz (Fr., Gm.) – A lively dance in $\frac{3}{4}$ time.